The U.S. Military's Rape of the Century

The U.S. Military's Rape of the Century
The Korean War's Forgotten Congressional Medal of Honor

By
Sergeant William Gibson
As told to Paula McCoy-Pinderhughes

Copyright © 2012 by William Gibson

ISBN: 978-0-578-09614-8

Commercial Avenue Publishers
Somerset, NJ 08873

All rights reserved. No part of this publication may be reproduced, stored in a retrieval system or transmitted, in any form, or by any means, electronic, mechanical, recorded, photocopied, or otherwise, without the prior written permission of both the copyright owner and the above publisher of this book, except by a reviewer who may quote brief passages in a review.

The scanning, uploading, and distribution of this book via the Internet or via any other means without the permission of the publisher is illegal and punishable by law. Please purchase only authorized electronic editions and do not participate in or encourage electronic piracy of copyrightable materials. Your support of the author's rights is appreciated.

Printed in the United States of America

*Dedicated to my parents,
Reverend D.L. and Snow Gibson*

Sergeant William Gibson

William Gibson served as Grand Marshall in three New Jersey parades, one in his hometown of New Brunswick, the other in the town of Highland Park where he received local recognition for his brave service to country and the third in Perth Amboy NJ where he continued to bestow military pride on the Garden State. At 82 years old, he is also a cancer survivor. However, his notoriety or unprecedented bravery during his time in the Korean War was not enough to gain the attention of the issuers of the Congressional Medal of Honor.

Contents

CHILDHOOD YEARS 11
A SOLDIER'S PREPARATION 16
AN UNFORTUNATE INCIDENT. 21
PINEVILLE KENTUCKY 23
OFF TO YOUNGSTOWN - THE SHOESHINE . 24
STOPOVER IN CLEVELAND 27
THE RECRUITER. 28
PASSING THE TEST FOR FORT DIX, NJ 31
THE ARMY CHAPLAIN 34
FORT LEE, VIRGINIA 38
SEGREGATION?—IN THE ARMY? 40
LEGEND HAS IT 42
OFF TO JAPAN. 44
CAPTAIN BRADLEY BIGGS 47
TOURING GIFU 50
INVASION OF THE SOUTH (KOREA) 52
PROUD TO SERVE WITH THE 24TH. 53
BULL WALKING. 59
LOB THE GRENADES 61
TRAPPED IN THE MINEFIELDS – THE
    ROAD TO THE MEDAL OF HONOR? . . . 64
OLD TRIPLE NICKLES 70
A GROUND SHAKING EXPERIENCE 74
BACK AT FORT DIX 77
THE REUNION 78
DANCING THE NIGHT AWAY 81
OFF TO CZECHOSLOVAKIA 83
FORT POLK - LOUISIANNA 86

FORT CAMPBELL KENTUCKY - AIRBORNE .92
THE JUMP MASTER 96
101ST AIRBORNE DIVISION AND
    THE KU KLUX KLAN................. 98
UNEXPECTED DISCOVERY 101
ARKANSAS SEGREGATION 103
IRAN................................. 105
NORTH CAROLINA AGRICULTURAL &
    TECHNICAL (A&T) - 1962............ 106
REAPING WHAT YOU SOW 109
THE GREEN BERET-THE 6TH SPECIAL
    FORCES / FORT BRAGG, NC.......... 110
HURT IN VIETNAM/ DEFECTIVE CHUTES. .116
THE OLD GULF WAR 119
BAD TÖLZ, GERMANY 1968 127
FORT DEVENS - MASSACHUSETTES....... 129
MEDALS & RECORD FOR
    SFC E-7 WILLIAM GIBSON 130

CHILDHOOD YEARS

It's a good thing I come from a long line of survivors. My grandmother, Nancy Carter Gibson lived for a total of 106 years and with all of her mental faculties intact. She was physically active, religious, loving, and strong. She would recount stories to the family about Abraham Lincoln's administration the same way we speak of any 21st century President. I would need to call upon her strength, conviction, confidence, faith and longevity during my tour of duty in the 'Forgotten War,' more commonly known as the Korean War and other U.S. military conflicts during my twenty-one years of service in the United States Army.

My family grew up proud in Grady, Alabama, about 25 miles south of Montgomery, strategically maneuvering our way around racism, which seemed to affect the lives of so many of the people we knew. Still, for my family and me, Grady was home. No matter what happened there, we could boast later on that within my home state, Rosa Parks, Joe Lewis, and Jesse Owens were born, later on making history in their own right. The capital city of Montgomery was also where America's Civil Rights struggles began. In the sanctuary of the Dexter Avenue King Memorial Baptist Church, plans for a boycott of Montgomery's bus system were first announced and subsequently implemented in response to the arrest of Rosa Parks for refusing to give up her seat to a white passenger on a city bus on December 1, 1955. Today, the Rosa Parks Library and Museum sits in the heart of downtown on Montgomery Street. It was also the first pulpit occupied full time by the Reverend Dr. Martin Luther King, Jr.

I was the ninth of twelve children born to Reverend D.L., and Snow Gibson, both sharecroppers in this tiny one-room schoolhouse town, where an education beyond the sixth grade for an African-American was virtually unheard of in 1939. And because we were a family of sharecroppers, I was only able to go to school when it rained, when I wasn't needed in the fields. Now, this didn't bother me so much, because more often than not, I was the only student in the classroom, and I would have the undivided attention of my teacher, Miss Rosy Taylor [sic], a full-blooded American Indian. Miss Taylor encouraged me to study hard. She always told me she knew in her heart I'd make it, although at times, it seemed nearly impossible to a young black boy.

As a child, my parents stressed that I shouldn't hang out with the local guys, especially when they were in large groups. They said if there was trouble to be found, the white law enforcement would not discriminate when it came to punishing black youth, innocent or not, we would all be assumed guilty first.

REVEREND D.L. and SNOW GIBSON

My family had a close relationship with our neighbors, the Nickerson, and Lawson families. They were good, respectable people. I remember fondly my parents telling me of weekend weight lifting contests that took place out in the countryside. We Gibson's would always win those matches along with our cousins, the Briders, a tall family, most of whom were at least six foot five, or some even closer to seven feet tall! There was one heroic story about how my paternal grandfather, Calvin Gibson, who was double jointed, tamed an unruly mule with his bare hands. One day the animal had become agitated, kicking and jerking for no apparent reason. Well, my grandfather gave it one good punch in the head and the mule never got up, never recovered. He was one man you did *not* want to cross!

I'm named for my maternal grandfather, William Norman, a well-respected and hardworking American Indian from the Cherokee Indian tribe. And like both my grandfathers, work for me began at an early age. By the time I'd reached 8-years old, I was already working in the fields, sun up to sun down, barely enough time left to play.

My father, Reverend D.L., who, as far back as I can remember, was always known by his initials, would lead prayer services at home at least once a week and would invite the neighbors to join us once a month.

Both my father and my uncle Eddie Lee Gibson, served honorably in the U.S. military during WWI in 1917 with the Buffalo Soldiers Division. The nickname 'Buffalo Soldier' dates back to the late 1860s, when black soldiers volunteered for duty in the American West. According to one story, American Indians coined the term 'Buffalo Soldier' because, they thought, black soldiers with their dark skin and curly hair, resembled buffaloes. Another story attributes the name to the buffalo hides that many black soldiers wore during the harsh winters out West as a supplement to their inadequate uniforms issued by the government. The 92nd Infantry Division was formed in November 1917 with African-American Selective Servicemen (Draftees). The 92nd was divided among several camps with Dodge, Dix, and Meade containing the largest units. One of the regiments in the division, the 366th Infantry Regiment, made up of men from Alabama, had the distinction of being the first all-black fighting unit to be commanded by black officers. Up until this point in time, black units had been commanded by white officers. The Buffalo Soldiers Division was one of the first organized units of the 367th Infantry division.

One of the last casualties of WWI was William M. Cain, an African-American soldier of the 92nd "Buffalo" Division, a soldier of the 366th Infantry Regiment who had come from my home state of Alabama to do his part in the great war for civilization.

A SOLDIER'S PREPARATION

It was 1948, two years before the North Korean troops crossed the 38th parallel and invaded South Korea. I was 18 years old and already preparing to answer the call of duty. During the 22 years I served on Active Duty, I was never drafted, I always volunteered. Even if I were needed today, at 82 years old, I would not hesitate to answer the call.

McKenzie, the third oldest child in my family, was already in the military, stationed at Camp Kilmer, in Edison New Jersey. He told me that racially, life was 'pretty fair' in the Garden State, and different from our small town in Grady, Alabama.

McKenzie and I were so different, almost opposites. I always managed to stay away from trouble; he seemed to gravitate towards it. He had a quick temper, I was much calmer. I would always advise him to think before acting. Sometimes he listened, most times he didn't. I believed in saving and investing, he never even considered it. Even so, I admired and respected him as my older brother. One thing we did have in common was the same birthday, and as brothers, we set a record as masons in the Progressive Lodge of New Brunswick, together, having a combined 118 years of service and membership. I joined Sims Lodge in Fort Campbell, Kentucky in 1957, he joined the Masonic Progressive Lodge in New Brunswick, NJ 1946. I demitted (transferred) to the Progressive Lodge 17 in New Brunswick in 1958.

One of the first *New Deal* programs of President Franklin D. Roosevelt included the Civilian Conservation Corps (CCC), a program designed to tackle the problem of unemployed young men between 18 and 25 years old. The CCC camps were set up all over the United States. The organization was fashioned after the armed forces with military officers in charge of the men. The pay was about $30 dollars a month. Men planted trees, built public parks, drained swamps to fight malaria, restocked rivers with fish, worked on flood control projects and a range of other work that helped conserve the environment. Between 1933 and 1941 over 3,000,000 men served in the CCCs. The army's experience in managing such large numbers and the paramilitary discipline learned by corpsmen provided unexpected preparation for the massive call-up of civilians during World War II. McKenzie actually joined the CCCs when he was just 15 years old, listing his age as three years older. He was referred to as the 'trailblazer' within my family circle.

At its peak, more than 250,000 African-Americans were enrolled in nearly 150 all-black CCC companies. After his entrance into the regular army, McKenzie was recognized and credited with 2 years of basic service for his time in the CCCs. He soon went into advanced infantry training and was stationed in India, where he, along with his good friend Alonzo Randolph, played a major role during WWII in blocking the Japanese entry through Kung Main China into India.

McKenzie worked for General Joseph Warren Stilwell, known to his men as "Vinegar Joe," because of his blunt candor, and at other times as "Uncle Joe" because of his willingness to share the hardships of the common soldier. When Japan forced the Allied withdrawal from Burma in May 1942, during WWII, Stilwell, at age 59, led a group of approximately 100 soldiers and civilians on a daring 140-mile march through the Burmese jungle and safely into India. He later commanded U.S. and Chinese forces in the conquest of Burma. Stilwell received his fourth star on August 1, 1944. After I joined the Green Berets in 1962, I had the honor of working for his son, Brigadier General Joseph Warren Stilwell, Jr.

Months would pass before my mother would hear any news from McKenzie. During one particular time, during vicious fighting abroad, I remember mother going into our prayer room after breakfast. I decided to follow her, but stopped quickly at the door. I knocked and asked for permission to enter. I could see that she'd been crying, and even at my young age, I reminded her of what she'd taught us. "Always have faith and believe in God," she would say. "If you do, everything will be ok." I said, "We can't worry about brother, we have to trust God." Mother always remembered that and was proud that I'd listened to what she'd often preached to her children. She even recited my young words to the congregants in church. Later on, mother received a partially burned letter from McKenzie, a possible indication that the mail plane could have been shot down. But to our great relief, he wasn't aboard that aircraft. Once again, mother recalled my comforting words and gained strength from them. I don't ever remember seeing her cry again.

GIBSON BROTHERS

My brother Eddie Lee, the fourth oldest child, took a different route. At 17-years old, he decided to go to work for the Atlantic Coastline Railroad that ran through Grady, Alabama. Although I was only about 12 years old at the time, Eddie Lee spoke to the railroad foreman and asked permission to bring me in for a work tryout. Surprisingly, the foreman agreed and began by teaching me the proper way to pick up weights. "Plant your feet solidly on the ground," he instructed. "Bend your knees, keep your back straight and your head up," he finished. I'd remember this simple lesson throughout my life. Early one Monday morning, the foreman marked off yards, assigning two men teams to replace the wooden cross-ties that supported the steel rails that trains ran on. Today, all this is done by machines. Wood is no longer used—all replaced by steel frames installed in non-decaying concrete. By noon, it was already hot. The temperature had reached above ninety degrees. The foreman blew his whistle for lunch. He called everyone over to the shaded area and told me to sit on top of a tall drum. He said, "Most of you men weigh more than 200 pounds. Eddie Lee and his younger brother William have already put in three crossties, more than any one of you. So, after lunch Eddie Lee, you just take it easy and throw up stones in low places to support the rail beds. William, you stay in the shade and when I blow the whistle, just bring out the water for the men." I laugh even now just thinking about that time. I worked there for about eight months.

AN UNFORTUNATE INCIDENT

One of my uncles, Floyd Norman and two of his sons, Floyd Jr. and James were working on the railroad in Georgia, near Atlanta, repairing train tracks. Uncle Floyd and his sons would come home to Grady about once every two weeks. I remember him asking my parents if I could go with him and his sons to Georgia because he knew I was an experienced, albeit young, railroad worker. My father agreed to let me go back with them after they'd returned from one of their weekend jobs.

But just prior to my going off with Uncle Floyd, he and his sons were caught in the middle of an unfortunate racial incident on the train back to Grady. Before boarding the train, a black man known around town as Little Bud Freeman had some unpleasant words with a white assistant train operator. As the train moved out and reached the crest, the assistant train operator disconnected the coach where Uncle Floyd, my cousins and most of the other black passengers sat, killing more than

200 people. You would have expected that an accident of this magnitude would have been investigated, but I don't recall ever reading anything about it in the news. I suspect it was a sign of the times and the fact that all of the victims were black. The only reason my cousin Floyd Jr. lived was because he'd decided to go to another car to talk with some friends.

PINEVILLE KENTUCKY

In 1942, at 12 years old, I asked for and was given permission from my parents to go and work with my uncle Vetenia Gibson, known to the family as Uncle Sing, on the L&N Railroad in Pineville Kentucky, a place mostly noted today for its Daniel Boon Wilderness Trail. Uncle Sing was a supervisor for the railroad. His boss, a man by the name of Mr. Holleyfield, [sic] was impressed by how effective I was at drilling spikes at such a young age and brought over the more seasoned workers to watch me. He offered me a promotion if I agreed to return the next year. Although I enjoyed my work there, what I really wanted was a steady job that would allow me to go to school. I stayed for the better part of a year before returning home to Grady.

OFF TO YOUNGSTOWN - THE SHOESHINE

Before the tragic accident of my uncle and cousins, mother had insisted that I prepare to go to Youngstown, Ohio and live with her cousins, most of whom were schoolteachers. She felt that by being in Youngstown, I'd have a better chance and an opportunity to finish school. Maybe, she thought, I would be able to attend school at night and work during the day. I dodged death, convinced that faith was working for me though my beloved mother, who I loved dearly and considered very special.

So after leaving Uncle Sing in Kentucky, I went to Youngstown to live with one of mother's cousins. I immediately decided it was time to look for work, but because of my young age, finding employment was difficult at best. One day, I visited the bus depot, a huge facility where buses came in from all over the United States. I noticed three men at a busy shoeshine stand. I approached the only African-American working there, a man named

Mr. Lampford, [sic] and asked if he thought I could get work. He said, "Sure, I would think so. Just go over and speak to the gentleman over there." He pointed to a well-dressed man wearing a tie. Mr. Lampford said the man was of Polish descent. That man was also shining shoes. I figured he was the boss, even before being told. He was a towering figure to a little boy. He looked to be about seven feet tall. Feeling a bit intimidated, I summoned up the nerve to ask if he would hire me. He turned to me and asked in a heavily accented voice, "Can you shine shoes?" I mustered up a solid, "Yes sir," confidently, respectfully, and unknowingly preparing for a lifetime of "yes sirs" during my career in the armed forces. I started work that same day and was told by my new employer to report to work every day at 8 o'clock in the morning.

Now in 1944, the cost of a shoeshine was fifteen cents, and the rule was that you'd put five cents in the kitty and keep the rest, including all your tips.

It didn't take long before everyone noticed that most of the customers waited for me to shine their shoes. I may have been young, but I was thorough, and always showed everybody respect. It ended up being that I could easily pay my cousin's $10 weekly room rent, even with my boss limiting my hours, because, it seemed, I was making so much more than everybody else. But I didn't mind. Even at my age, I understood how things worked in the world of small business.

Military personnel made up the majority of the customers passing through the bus depot. I'll always remember the time, after just a couple of days on the job, a Navy Lieutenant Commander and a Petty Officer standing near a corner of the shop, waiting their turn. One of the available shoe shiners asked if they would like to sit down at his station. "No," the Lieutenant Commander said, "we're waiting for the kid."

Once he sat down at my station, I noticed his shoes were already shiny, but I went to work anyway. Afterwards, I shined the Petty Officer's shoes. When I finished, the Lieutenant Commander went into his pocket and pulled out a money clip filled with bills. He handed me $83. The Petty Officer gave me $53. You might imagine how stunned a kid back then would have been to get that kind of money. The ranking officer then suggested I get permission from my boss to go and open up a savings account. He asked whether I'd completed high school. I told him I hadn't, but that I intended on finishing. He encouraged me to go to night school and consider joining the military, assuring me that if I studied hard, he had no doubt that I'd do well. He even suggested that I meet with an army recruiter, someone who could tell me the names of the books I'd need for passing the military entrance exam. "If you get into the army," the Commander said with conviction, "I know you'll make it." I thanked him for his advice and just a few years later did just as he'd suggested. I remember that story with pride and salute the wisdom of those two men.

After putting five dollars in the kitty and sharing some of my windfall with the other two workers, I rushed over to the bank and opened a savings account. I was able to pay my rent two months in advance! I laugh about that time even today because I'm quite sure that I still hold the shoeshine tip record in Youngstown, Ohio.

STOPOVER IN CLEVELAND

I lived and worked in Youngstown for the better part of a year before moving on to Cleveland to join my sister, Ester Bell and her husband, Sammie Gamble. One of Sammie's three brothers, Oscar, who was about 5 feet 11 inches tall and 165 pounds was discovered playing baseball in a semi-professional league by Buck O'Neil, a batting champion in the legendary Negro Leagues, who at the time was working as a scout for the Chicago Cubs. In 1969, O'Neil convinced the Cubs to draft Oscar, who later went on to have a 17-year major league career with the Chicago Cubs, Philadelphia Phillies, Cleveland Indians, and the New York Yankees. He was nicknamed the 'Big O' by Yankees announcer, Phil Rizzuto. Oscar also played for the Chicago White Sox, San Diego Padres, and the Texas Rangers. Oscar hit 200 career home runs in just over 4500 major league at bats. The Gamble brothers, who by the way were originally from Ramer, Alabama were all gifted ball players.

THE RECRUITER

Once I arrived in Cleveland, I was able to secure a part-time job working in a defense plant. I remained on the job for about six months. My duties included picking up and moving heated engine parts using special heat resistant gloves and then unloading them to a new location. But because of the demanding hours, it was difficult to go to school at night. I contacted my brother McKenzie, who by now had completed his tour in India and was stationed at Fort Benning, Georgia shortly before being sent back to Camp Kilmer in Edison, New Jersey. I wanted to know if he thought I'd find opportunities there. He assured me I would. Soon afterwards, I left Cleveland.

Remembering what I'd been told by the Navy Commander while shining his shoes, I visited the army recruiting station in New Brunswick where a recruiter offered reading suggestions in books that would prepare me for taking the required test for entry into the military.

"When you're not working," he said, "always keep your head in the books." I did just that—reading everything I could get my hands on. I'd gotten a job working for the Pennsylvania Railroad, lining and replacing cross- ties. When I wasn't working, I spent my time in the library, studying math and English. I was determined to complete my high school education. The recruiter told me that he had no doubt that if I continued to study as I'd been doing, I'd be prepared to take the test within the next few months. He informed me that the test consisted mostly of pattern analysis, division, and grammar and that's what I studied.

After a couple of months, I went in to take the test feeling very prepared. There were two Caucasian kids there from Rutgers University. One was a sophomore, the other, a second semester freshman. Now you might wonder why two college kids would want to leave school and risk their lives in the armed services. I can't say for certain, however, I truly believe that this is the fiber from which Americans are made. We are and always have been patriots when it comes to defending our country. Black, white, brown and all races of men and women are proud Americans who would never run away from a fight, no matter how young or old—we sprint towards it. That's my belief.

The instructor told us that after we complete the test, stand up to signify that we were done and wait outside the classroom while he graded the papers. Later on he said to me, "To my knowledge, you never attended Rutgers University, right?" I said, "No sir."

"Well," he continued, "I want you to know that you

made a better score than the college kids." I couldn't believe it. I was elated. He reminded me again to stay out of trouble and prepare to enter the military. I left there beaming and immediately enrolled in school to attend night classes.

PASSING THE TEST FOR FORT DIX, NJ

I told my oldest sister, D. L. Gibson Walton, who was named after my father, that I'd passed the test and now had a steady home in the army. Although she was jubilant, I told her not to tell anyone else, not even my oldest brother, McKenzie. I just wanted the news to come from me, to be a pleasant surprise for the family. But the more I thought about it and knowing my sister, everybody probably already knew.

On the morning of January 3, 1949, I went down to Patterson Street in New Brunswick, NJ and boarded the bus to Fort Dix where new recruits were being processed. I was assigned to the 1st Battalion 'C' Company, First Platoon where I was established as squad leader shortly after going on duty. The first question I asked of my Platoon Sergeant was how I could attend night school. I was told that as soon as I got completely set up, that it would be taken care of. Once everything was in place for school, I didn't care if we'd already spent a couple of training hours running in the mud, I'd go back to my quarters, take a shower, eat and then attend classes. I was determined to continue and complete my education.

During one of our first work details, the 1st Platoon Sergeant asked for any personnel who had a driver's license, and were authorized to operate automobile vehicles, to step forward. Practically everyone, except for me, stepped forward. I stood right where I was, I didn't move. He said, "I see we only have one smart man here, and I can see why I selected Gibson as team leader." Everybody looked around at me, puzzled. They didn't quite understand what was going on at first, but soon figured it out. When the men reached the airfield, there was a truck loaded with wheelbarrows. The Sergeant dismounted his truck, pointed to me and said, "Gibson, you stand over there, everyone else, fall in on your leader," meaning me. The men did as they were told and he continued his commands. "Gibson, march your men over to the truck and have the driver give everyone a wheelbarrow." You see, there were drivers needed to drive specific types of vehicles to unload two C-36 planeloads of large slabs of Texas choice beef and bring them to freezers where other men were assigned to hang up the meat for later use. While everyone else was assigned a wheelbarrow for unloading heavy beef, I was invited to hang out with the Platoon Sergeant. This backbreaking operation lasted about eight hours. I'd given instructions that the men were to take a 10-minute break every hour just to catch their breath and get a drink of water before resuming their duties. There was no movie night after that day's work. The soldiers were too exhausted.

THE ARMY CHAPLAIN

During my time in basic training, I'd seemingly walk for miles at a time and spent hours at the range familiarizing myself with my assigned mark weapon, practicing shooting. While there, I met a distant cousin with the last name of Gibson, but whose first name escapes me, and who happened to be the highest-ranking black officer in the army in my area. A Lieutenant Colonel, he was originally from Pennsylvania. Most of the Gibson's you meet are in some way distantly related. Lt. Colonel Gibson was a fair-skinned man, looking more Hispanic, than black. He said to me, "I know we're related and I'll bet I can even tell you where our ancestors landed on these shores." Oh boy, I thought, he's sharp.

As I reminisce about that time with my cousin, I'm reminded of a story of when I was stationed in Korea in an area known as Battle Mountain, or as we called it, 'Bloody Peak.' A group of young men, maybe twenty or thirty of them, were refusing to go up on line for a mission. It wasn't because they were afraid to fight, no, it was only that they'd already heard about the many who'd died before them, and they wanted and needed to talk to a Chaplain before heading out. Normally, the Chaplain would have been the one to call, but because he was unavailable, they sent for the other Gibson, me. I was already aware that the men knew and admired my cousin and I was told that their moral was low. So to see someone other than the Chaplain, in my mind, could have done more harm than good. I began by telling them my name and that I was proud to be the distant cousin of the Chaplain. "Let me tell you a little bit about myself," I said. I told them where I was from and that I was the son of sharecroppers and proud to say that I was working my way through school while serving my country. "My objective is to do good things in life," I said, reminding them that although some were older and probably wiser than I was, like them, I had many loved ones back home—parents, sisters, brothers, and cousins that I wanted to get back home to. I said that I looked forward to going back home when this was all over and that once I returned home, I wanted to be able to look my loved ones squarely in the eyes and salute them, because I'd be going back not in disgrace, but having accomplished something great. I reminded them of the oath we'd taken before enlisting, which, as they would recall, held that we would obey all orders given to us by our Commanders. "I'm realistic," I said bluntly. "I know that when we go out, all of us won't return. But believe in the Almighty and keep the faith. Envision going home when it's all over." I finished by saying that if I were instructed to join them on their mission, I wouldn't hesitate one moment. "Would I be afraid? Yes, of course," I admitted. "But I have the courage to do the job I was assigned to do. And not only will I confront the enemy, I'll defeat him."

They seemed genuinely impressed by my candor. "Now those of you who choose to go home other than proud and brave soldiers, raise your hand." No one did. "You see," I said, "the reason our country is free is because of the many people who well before we were ever thought of, gave their lives for what we are enjoying back in the states." One of the soldiers raised his hand and said, "But when we go back home, we still have to sit at the back of the bus." I let him know that I was well aware of that, but that I felt it would all be corrected by the time we returned because of the work and dedication of the great Martin Luther King, Jr.

"He's on the firing line back there for you and I and we're here for him, our loved ones, and our country. And if any of you have any hesitation about doing your job—you'll automatically go back in disgrace."

I knew in my heart that none of them wanted to go to Leavenworth, Kansas (the army prison) in chains. "Now, you don't have to agree with me, but think about it, you have one mission here and that's to defeat the enemy. Think of the leaders who've given their lives, just as we may be asked to do. So hold your head high as brave soldiers who love their country and do as you're instructed." I felt good after that speech, as if somehow I'd made a difference in some young soldier's life. I learned later on that one of those young men went on to win the Battlefield Commission, awarded to enlisted soldiers promoted to the rank of commissioned officer for outstanding leadership on the battlefield. He went there and did it all. And as I think on it now, had I been given the recognition of the Congressional Medal of Honor, I would also have qualified for the Battlefield Commission. I was respected within the division for having given that inspirational speech, but I was also kidded. The Officers would say, 'If you can't get the Chaplain when we need him, just call Gibson.'

SISTERS, MOTHER AND BROTHER

FORT LEE, VIRGINIA

From Fort Dix I was transferred to Fort Lee, Virginia where I was still able to attend night courses on base every night. After being observed by the Company Commander, 1st Sergeant, and the Platoon leaders, all of whom were African-American, I was placed in charge of the drill team. I would read over my schedule to see what my Platoon leader assigned. I would be instructed to study a particular chapter in the manual, highlighting what was important or needed, such as stressing the importance of nutrition, limiting the use of alcoholic beverages, running for five miles before dinner or performing calisthenics. To accomplish this, your body had to be in top shape. If the men were not up to par, then they were off the drill team. I would confer commands such as: 'Drill Team/Drill Platoon, attench-hut, right face,' using different vocal cords or vocalizations. I'd continue with, 'Dress right Dress' a movement where soldiers would raise their left arms parallel to the ground and lock their heads to the far right in order to get the proper distance from each other. This was maintained until the command, 'Ready Front,' at which point, the individuals returned to the position of attention. All this was done with precision, automatically and without much thought. I'd then give maybe two other commands: Right Shoulder, ARMS. Order, ARMS. Left shoulder, arms. Then I'd end with: Situation one, starting position move. Company, attench-hut. Everyone knew exactly what they were to do. I would continue giving commands until the impressive drill was completed. But after only eight months, I became restless. I wanted, if not needed, new and exciting adventures. Even with all of my added responsibilities and the positive responses I'd received for my professional capacity, I was ready to go. It seems that I was always on the move, no matter the danger that lay ahead. I'd always remember hearing from my dad and uncle that there was a whole world outside of Grady to be discovered and explored, and I intended to take full advantage of the opportunities I was given. I immediately volunteered for an overseas assignment.

One day, while outside in formation, the Platoon Sergeant called out, "Squad Leader Gibson, front and center." I appeared on the double. "How long will it take you to pack up?" he asked. "Give me about 40 minutes sir and I'll be ready," I answered. He threw his hands up in the air and said, "No, no, no, you can take a couple of days. You're going to Japan."

"Yes sir," I answered, "that's fine."

SEGREGATION?— IN THE ARMY?

When I joined the army in 1949, I was young, only eighteen years old and really didn't understand the polarization of racism. I naively thought that when you were shipped overseas and engaged in combat, you and your fellow soldiers went in as members of the *United States* Army. I was immediately given a healthy dose of reality.

After going into advanced training I met my cadre, a group of WWII veterans who filled me in on what to expect. "You know," they said, "the *enemy* doesn't care what color you are, all they want to do is kill you for being an *American* soldier, not because you are a black or white soldier. But to the American military, you're a black soldier in a white army." And to my disappointment during that time, I found out that no truer words were ever spoken.

I really had no idea of what I was in for. However, I was aware of the segregation of soldiers during basic training because all of the African-American soldiers were located on Range Road at Fort Dix, (where the Mid-State Correctional Facility sits today). But what I didn't realize was how segregated the army was overseas. It was in 1948 when President Harry S. Truman ordered Executive Order 9981, the desegregation of U.S. forces, but it would take until 1951 before all units were fully integrated.

Nevertheless, I was proud to be an American, and an American soldier, even though African-Americans still suffered countless inequalities back at home. I can recall the pride I felt upon learning that a black engineering group built most of the major roadways and most of the runways at Pope Air Force Base, located on the northern edge of the city of Fayetteville, North Carolina. And, I was told, that same African-American group built most of Fort Dix, and half of the roadway to Alaska. I also learned that a Caucasian engineering unit started at one end of the roadway and set a deadline for completion but weren't able to finish on time. The African-American unit's schedule was kept, and met. Although this knowledge couldn't make up for the pain of segregation, it felt good to learn of just some of our contributions and accomplishments.

LEGEND HAS IT

African-American's played a major role in building the railroads and highways in the U.S.

John Henry, a former slave, who some say was from Virginia, but who my paternal grandmother stated with absolute authority that he was from Alabama, was a legendary railroad worker known as the 'steel-drivin' man during the 1870s. He worked between 1870 and 1872 as a hammer man or steel driver during construction of the Big Bend (or Great Bend) Tunnel on the Chesapeake & Ohio Railroad near the Greenbrier River in Summers County, in Talcott, West Virginia. These men used sledgehammers to drive long steel bits into treacherous red shale to bore the holes for the explosives that would open the tunnel. It took a thousand men and boys three years to finish. But legend has it that John Henry beat the steam powered drill machine in a famous contest that took place right at Great Bend Tunnel. The story goes that one day, a salesman with a steam-powered drill claimed it could out-drill any man. When the owner of the railroad bought the steam-powered drill to do the work of his mostly black driving crew, John Henry, in order to save his job and the jobs of his men, challenged the owner to a contest: himself alone versus the steam hammer. A contest was set up between John Henry and the drill. The foreman ran the new steam-drill while John Henry pulled out two 20-pound hammers, one in each hand. The drilling began. Dust rose everywhere. Men cheered him on. Half an hour later, John Henry had drilled two seven-foot holes - a total of fourteen feet, while the steam drill had only drilled one nine-foot hole. John Henry held up his hammers in triumph as the men shouted and cheered. But exhausted from drilling, John Henry crashed to the ground, both hammers rolling from his hands. The foreman rushed to his side. But it was too late. A blood vessel had burst in his brain. The greatest driller in the Chesapeake & Ohio Railroad was dead. This story and others like it only deepened my sense of dignity and pride.

OFF TO JAPAN

It was 1950. It took more than a month to reach Japan aboard the great transport, General Nelson M. Walker, carrying about 5000 soldiers aboard ship. We visited several ports and were caught in numerous storms losing much-needed lifeboats, which could each hold up to 300 people. The secure cables holding the boats, about 5 inches in diameter, roughly the size of a fruit jar, were no match for the storm. During one of those storms, the ship crashed with large waves from side to side. I think everyone aboard thanked God it somehow remained upright. At least three times one night the ship's compartment doors began closing, causing bright red lights to flash, and sirens to blast indicating a dangerous level of submersion. With no air conditioning like today's ships, and the swaying of the immense vessel, men became ill, vomiting everywhere. The smell was unbearable, but we made it through the storm, losing only one boat. After making stops at several seaports, the ship finally arrived at Yokahoma seaport near the town of Osaka, Japan.

General Nelson M. Walker

Once we disembarked, and were offloaded onto buses and trucks and headed to our final destination of Gifu, Japan. Three years before the war began, commanders stationed a regiment at Gifu, Japan, which sits 370 miles southwest of Tokyo, on the main island of Honshu. Gifu was where my unit of the 24th Infantry Regimental Combat team, the 'Deuce-Four,' last of the Buffalo Division, and the largest black unit to serve in Korea was stationed. I learned later that my unit was the unit my father and uncle served in during WWI with pride.

Gifu Prefecture sits northeast of Osaka and occupied the former Japanese airfield of Kagamigahara, then known by the U.S. Army as Camp Majestic, the former camp of the 27th Infantry Regiment. It was renamed Camp Gifu upon the arrival of the 24th Infantry. Yokahoma was a port used by the U.S. Navy as a transshipment base for supplies and personnel before being transported to Gifu, Japan. I was assigned to the 24th Infantry Regimental Combat Team, "L" (Love) Company of the 25th Infantry Division, as assistant squad leader. I taught infantry squad tactics. The unit was commanded by Bradley Biggs, a Tuskegee Airmen during WWII. Biggs joined the infantry and became Company Commander of the 24th Infantry, L Company.

CAPTAIN BRADLEY BIGGS

Captain Bradley Biggs was one of the first black officers accepted for parachute duty in the U.S. Army and a member of the 555th Battalion of the 82nd Airborne. He had previously served with the Tuskegee Airman during WWII. During the Korean War, Captain Biggs, a member of the renowned 555th Paratroop Division, noted that they were given particularly dangerous combat duties. In 1986, he authored a book, "The Triple Nickles," which memorialized the unit's struggles and historic achievements. Biggs was born in Newark, NJ, and enlisted with the U.S. Army after high school. He later rose to the rank of Lt. Colonel, after making history as the first African-American soldier accepted into the Army's elite paratrooper unit. After WWII ended, Captain Biggs joined the 24th Infantry Regimental Combat Team, the Buffalo Division as Company Commander after his airborne duties. He said this of the 24th. *"The 24th Infantry Regiment deserves to be remembered as the unit that brought into focus the enormous price in blood and treasure the United States paid for its national and military indulgence in racism. With unmistakable clarity, the 24th Infantry Regiment exposed the folly of military and civilian leaders who prolonged the absurdity of a segregated army. In this way, the men of the 24th Infantry Regiment hastened integration. Above all else, this is the Deuce-Four's legacy."*

Colonel Biggs and his family moved to Middletown, NJ in 1967 at the invitation of fellow Army veteran Phillip Wheaton, the founding President of Middlesex Community College, to assist in the College's start-up and management. Col. Biggs held several positions at the college over the next decade, including Dean of Faculty and Dean of Administration. Subsequently, Col. Biggs served as the State of Connecticut's Deputy Commissioner of Public Works; as C.E.O. of the Boston Housing Authority; and on the faculty of Florida International University in Miami. Col. Biggs died in 2004 of heart failure in Middletown, NJ. He was 83 years old. I felt he was one of the best leaders in the army.

The prominent Oliver W. Dillard, today a retired Army 2-star General had been in Gifu and was assigned to the company under Bradley Biggs. Dillard became Commander of the 3rd Platoon with 'L' Company, 3rd Battalion after Biggs was injured. "A short while after I was in Korea, I received a radio call from Lt. Colonel Pierce that Commander Biggs had fallen and had to be sent back to the rear," General Dillard remembered with specificity. He was ordered to take over 'L' company. "I never saw Biggs again during combat," Dillard recalled.

And while in Haman, Korea, the General himself ended up being injured and was sent back to Japan.

TOURING GIFU

We arrived in Gifu on a weekend and were told that we could immediately go on weekend pass to socialize. We were instructed to wear our stateside insignias, and to try to stay away from hard liquor and trouble. 'Try not to get drunk,' the officers advised. 'Drink a beer, if you want,' they'd say. 'And remember that General Douglas MacArthur was well respected here and because of that, you should have few problems from the Japanese people.' I decided to ride a city bus to the end of the line and back as a way of familiarizing myself with the area. At some point during my ride, a young lady, possibly a college student came aboard. She was seated diagonally from where I sat. I noticed her watching me. Finally, she asked, in broken, but understandable English, "What company you?" I kept a straight face and answered, "I'm from Q Company." Knowing full well there was no such company. She said, "You make me pissed as a B-29," a reference to the Boeing B-29 Super fortress, known to be the plane that dropped the atomic bombs on the Japanese cities of Hiroshima and Nagasaki, which essentially ended World War II. It was also used in the war effort during the Korean War.

"MacArthur!" she yelled, her way of swearing, like saying 'go to hell.' I was astonished. Now I'd read how the Japanese equated the B-29 with MacArthur, but I just couldn't believe that I was witnessing it first hand, here on a city bus. I said apologetically, "Please excuse me, there's no such unit as a 'Q' Company. I'm actually assigned to 'L' Company of the 24th Infantry Regimental Combat Team."

"You didn't have to lie," she said angrily. I laughed and said, "Oh, I was just kidding with you. And I want you to know that you look beautiful, even when you're angry." I really enjoyed meeting some of the local people.

INVASION OF THE SOUTH (KOREA)

Six months after being stationed in Gifu, in 1950, Kim Il Sung, the leader of North Korea, invaded South Korea, including the capital of Seoul with the full force of his army, approximately 900,000 men with the approval of China and the Soviet Union. My Company Commander asked if anyone wanted to transfer. I immediately answered, 'wherever I'm needed, I'm there sir.' I was told that the Regimental Commander had observed me as squad leader during tactical training. He'd been impressed by my skills and work ethic and had instructed the Headquarter Service Company to keep tabs on me.

PROUD TO SERVE WITH THE 24TH

'L' Company of the 24th Infantry Regiment, 25th Infantry Division, U.S. Eighth Army, arrived in Korea to fight in a war that then Army Chief of Staff General Omar N. Bradley said was, "the wrong war, in the wrong place, at the wrong time and with the wrong enemy." The 24th Infantry Regiment was ill equipped for combat. 'L' Company landed without any light machineguns, 60-millimeter (mm) mortars, Browning automatic rifles, or bazooka antitank weapons, which had been standard equipment in World War II. There are still those who would tell you that the soldiers of the 24th were not qualified or ready for combat. But I'm living proof that they were brave and more than qualified officers and soldiers.

In July, 1950, the 3rd Battalion, 24th Infantry supported by other elements of the 24th Regimental Combat Team conducted the first major offensive mission of the 25th Infantry Division with its recapture of the vital road junction town of Yech'on, driving out the North Korean defenders and repulsing a North Korean attempt to retake the town. It was considered by Congress and the Department of Defense as the first sizeable American ground victory of the war.

After the invasion of the 'Pusan Perimeter,' at Yech'on, a young African-American Captain by the name of Charles M. Bussey, who was also a World War II Tuskegee Airman, made history by earning a Silver Star for his service and bravery during a conflict with a large group of North Korean soldiers disguised as peasants. Bussey, who was Commander of the Engineering Company supporting the 24th, noticed the group of North Koreans trying their best to outflank the 24th. Wounded twice during the ensuing battle, Bussey was able to stop them cold, mowing down more than 200 North Korean soldiers.

Once my unit landed, we'd get in position, ready to fight. The 24th Infantry fought throughout the entire Korean peninsula. From the defense of the Pusan Perimeter to its breakout and the pursuit of communist forces well into North Korea, to the Chinese counteroffensives, and finally to U.N. counteroffensives that stabilized near the current Demilitarized Zone (DMZ), we'd keep pushing, driving out the North Korean defenders and repulsing any attempts to retake the towns. The Regiment received the Republic of Korea Presidential Unit Citation for its defense of the Pusan Perimeter, however, the all-black unit was inactivated effective October 1, 1951 at Chipo-ri, Korea after six Korean War campaigns and 85 years of continuous service in the United States

Army because ultimately, white policy makers realized that as the leader of the free world, America could no longer afford to openly and militarily discriminate against more than 10 percent of its population purely on the basis of race.

The regiment had two posthumous Medal of Honor recipients, Sergeant Cornelius H. Charlton and Private First Class William Thompson. Sergeant Charlton, initially assigned to an engineering group, requested transfer to an infantry unit and was subsequently placed in Company 'C' of the 24th Infantry Regiment, 25th Infantry Division. While attempting to take a hill near Seoul, his platoon leader was wounded. Charlton led the men on an assault against the hill and was subsequently wounded by a grenade. He refused medical attention and continued to lead the charge, single handedly attacking and disabling the last remaining enemy gun emplacement while suffering another grenade wound in the process. Charlton succumbed to his wounds, dying at the young age of 21. For his actions during the battle, he was awarded the Congressional Medal of Honor.

William Henry Thompson was the first enlisted man in the Korean War to receive the Congressional Medal of Honor. A slightly built kid, Thompson was raised by his grandmother in the tenements of New York before running away and making the Home for Homeless Boys in the Bronx his permanent residence. After drifting for a while, he decided to join the army and after only eight days after his arrival on foreign soil was faced with fanatical enemy forces who launched a surprise attack on his unit. Private First Class William Thompson, 24th

Infantry Regiment Company M, 25th Infantry Division, set up his machine gun in the path of the onslaught and swept the enemy with withering fire, pinning them down momentarily and permitting the remainder of his platoon to withdraw to a more defensible position. Although he was hit repeatedly by grenade fragments and small arms fire, he remained at his machine gun and continued to deliver deadly fire until wounded by an enemy grenade in August, 1950 near Haman, Korea. He died of his wounds two weeks later, just after his 23rd birthday.

There were other units in Korea as well. Two that I recall were the 35th and the 27th Infantry Regimental Combat teams, both of whom were white units. The 27th, known as the Wolfhounds, were later redeployed to the Territory of Hawaii in 1954. The 27th Wolfhounds were led by Lt. Colonel John H. 'Iron Mike' Michaelis. During World War II, Michaelis had commanded a regiment of the 101st Airborne Division in Holland. In Korea, he would receive two battlefield promotions within six months to full Colonel and Brigadier General.

A black tank unit formed a combat reinforced infantry platoon. The 24th had taken Seoul a second time, crossing the Han River near Seoul and blocking it when the enemy tried to get away. Douglas MacArthur, supreme commander in the Korean War had come during that time and I was fortunate to be able to see him.

The 3rd Battalion had been ordered to attack Yech'on and take it back from the North Koreans. Spotter planes would spot the enemy bringing in thousands of reinforcements, reinforcements we didn't' have, yet we would take Battle Mountain, hold it until the Sr. Commander would order a withdrawal, executing a retrograde movement in which we'd give it back to them, burn it up, kill the enemy, and go back and take it again.

But compounding the earlier problems of training, or lack thereof for the men of the 24th was the fact that the black soldiers of the 24th had not received any new equipment since World War II, and without armor, effective antitank weapons, or air support, they were being asked to hold the line against two divisions of well armed and motivated North Korean troops. Because our clothing was defective, I still to this day have medical problems with my feet. A lot of my buddies suffered from toe and foot amputations, but we still held our ground, killing more than 250 North Koreans at a cost of two dead and a handful of wounded.

No one can dispute the fact that the 24th Infantry achieved the first victory of the war, which gained national prestige, with headlines like *'Black Unit Wins First US Victory In Korea,'* though it wasn't remembered for very long. General Matthew B. Ridgway, UN Supreme Commander in Korea, under whose command I served, is on record as stating, "African-Americans were not given the credit some individuals and some units deserved for their service rendered in combat in Korea." General Ridgeway was a distinguished Commander and one of the few who wore hand grenades everywhere, hanging from his body like apples! We'd joke that if we came under enemy fire, to make damn sure you weren't anywhere near him.

In 1950, the 25th Infantry Division's commander, Major General William B. Kean, falsely recommended to 8th Army Headquarters that the 24th Infantry Regimental

Combat Team be relieved of frontline combat service. This recommendation was ignored by General Douglas MacArthur and subsequently, the record shows that the 24th fought as well as, if not better than other American regiments during the remainder of its last tour of duty.

BULL WALKING

After going into combat in Korea in 1950, I asked the Commanding officer if I could get any weapon I wanted instead of the World War II vintage M-1 rifles that were worn out, some even lacking firing pins. Several Companies didn't even have the basic materials they needed such as Browning Automatic Rifles, 4.2-inch mortars, light machine guns, and rocket launchers, along with the required ammunition.

I asked for the Browning Automatic Rifle (BAR), even though it was about 10 pounds heavier than the rifle. I knew it would pay off when I faced the enemy. I carried the BAR and an initial forty round clip instead of the normal eight that came in the rifle. I taped two clips together for a total of 80 rounds. I carried two 80 round clips in the front, two in the back, one on each side and one in the weapon. This was a lot of extra work and weight, but it was worth it. Every 4th round was a tracer, I didn't have to worry about sighting it. I used burst-on-target (BoT). You could put a tank outside here in New Brunswick, NJ, pick out a steeple several miles away in Edison, NJ and I could climb on top, adjust my sight and hit the target on the second shot. That's how good the method was.

I'd asked for action and that's exactly what I got. I was pulled back with the special squad and directed to set up a reconnaissance unit for when people went out to where they would encounter a fight. My name had been suggested as a dependable soldier. I recall an incident while we were on the Pusan Perimeter. The enemy had begun firing on some of our men. They were in grave danger.

They eventually opened up on the rest of us. I instructed everybody to get down by the vehicles. I told them that I was moving up the mountain. I then maneuvered up about 40 or 50 yards and said, 'When I open up, I want you all to start 'bull walking with the 81-mm mortar.' It's known in the military as 'Bull Walking.'

I said, 'When I start up, I want all of you to fire, but make sure you keep your fire up because I don't want to give the enemy a target. I'll be practically crawling. Fire over my head and when I open up, stop, and open up with the mortars.'

I went almost straight up the hill, still crawling down low on my stomach, listening to the enemy's bullets firing. I cut down small tree blades with the Browning rifle, opening up and emptying about 80 rounds on the enemy before putting in another clip. That gun was something else. The enemy took off, withdrawing and disappearing in the hills, breaking up the ambush. I then instructed the unit to hold their fire and stop bull walking with the mortars.

LOB THE GRENADES

In April, 1951, the enemy had successfully surrounded Haman, Korea. I'd already set up about five boxes of hand grenades around the area. We were on the move up front. 'Bravo' Situation was now in effect. Two Caucasian kids had brought up a radio mounted on a 2½-ton truck, a special radio with the ability to communicate all the way back to Japan if something happened. We were anticipating an enemy breakthrough. Sending them up during the daylight hours allowed us to know exactly where we needed to call in the fighter aircraft to drop bombs and block the enemy, subsequently getting the ammunition out. However, the enemy had already anticipated our move. They'd come down hours before, seemingly with the strength of a thousand men surrounding us. But it was my job to make sure they didn't get control of the ammunition.

We had one machine gun on the truck. I told the kids that we would protect the truck, so be ready to open up with the machine gun once we all opened up. "We're gonna hold this area even though they've surrounded us," I said. "Toss the grenades upon my command and under no circumstance should you surrender, because if you do, I'll shoot you first. We're gonna fight, so let 'em come in." I could hear the enemy talking. I could see their sheer numbers. There were enough of them there to eat us! They looked liked moving bushes. The kids asked me if I thought we'd make it out alive. I said "Sure," hoping to rein in their waning confidence. "Everything will be okay tomorrow morning. You'll even laugh about it once it's over."

I had taken seven of our trucks that were loaded with ammunition and pulled the pins halfway out of the grenades, leaving them on the seat of the trucks without anyone's knowledge. I told the men not to go near them until they checked with me. I would go there first. "If I'm killed," I told them later, "I want you to know that I booby-trapped the trucks with grenades."

An enemy fired on a truck and made his way over to it after concluding what he thought was a safe situation. He opened the door and the grenade pin went off. That particular truck was loaded with several flares that when lit up, turned night into day.

All the enemy had to do was keep coming. They were about 40 yards from us and we were certainly outnumbered. But once the truck flares went up, they started running for the bushes and hills. I said to my men, "Follow me and open up. Lob the grenades." But once they'd headed for the bushes and trees, we had to stop. They were too far away for a direct hit. I got everybody

LOB THE GRENADES

back safely and regrouped, preparing for the next attack.

The next morning I was told that the Regimental Commander wanted to see me. Once he arrived, one of the Caucasian kids who had brought up the radio mounted on a truck was also there and said, "Glad to see you, Colonel." The Regimental Commander said with a smirk, "You know, you're a *bad* boy."

"No sir," I replied, "You've got me all wrong, I'm a *good* boy." He laughed and said, "I've got some good reports on you, Corporal Gibson." Then the kid said to the Regimental Commander, "Sir, take that bird off your cap and collar and put it on the Corporal. He's fit to wear it." But sadly, I never received any official or formal recognition for my actions.

TRAPPED IN THE MINEFIELDS – THE ROAD TO THE MEDAL OF HONOR?

Four months before President Truman integrated the army, I was given the mission to make sure that ammunition did not fall into enemy hands. I received word by radio to take the ammunition train, a line of moving vehicles, and follow the 27th Infantry Regimental Combat Team, of the 1st Battalion, more commonly referred to as the 27th Wolfhounds, 200-300 yards out of Bloody Peak. This was a hilly area in Haman, Korea. Once you came down the hill, you could maneuver your way around the enemy. But by the time I came up and over, nobody was there. I moved out slowly. As I proceeded through the valleys, I found out that the enemy had snuck in during the night and mined the last hundred yards. We simply didn't have enough troops to guard the road. They had booby-trapped land mines approximately 100 yards off the last exit off the mountain.

The 27th Wolfhounds, led by Lieutenant Colonel John Michaelis, who I thought looked a little like the retired, red-haired, freckled faced, Mets baseball star, Rusty Staub, led his men from the front, choosing not to send his Lieutenants and Senior non-commissioned officers up front, something most senior leaders don't do—they prefer to send their officers out ahead of them.

Once I entered the minefield, everybody stopped. I could hear people hollering, 'take cover,' and yelling, 'you're in a minefield, get down, we've already had people killed.' The enemy began shooting huge 140-mm baseball-sized Russian made mortars. I ordered the people with the ammunition train to get down and take cover. We had been taught in basic training to size up the situation quickly before starting any action.

I began maneuvering for one of our own ammunition trucks, carrying my Browning automatic machine gun instead of the traditionally issued M-1 rifle. After safely reaching the truck, I climbed inside and laid low. Now, all you had to do was start moving around to guarantee a direct hit, which is precisely why I yelled out to the men, 'hit the ground and stay there.' The enemy fired every gun they had at me for about 100 yards, luckily missing me every time. I could hear the fire right near my ammunition-loaded vehicle, nonetheless, I started it up and reflected on my religious upbringing and what I'd been taught by my parents, which was to construct a makeshift cross wherever you were and put it at the Almighty's feet. I thought to myself, 'go ahead, do what you have to do.' So I backed the truck out the same way I thought it'd gone in—straddling the left tire rut out of the narrow road and zigzagging from left to right. I truly believe the Almighty made it possible for me to miss those landmines. I still get chills to this day when I think about it.

As I eased down the rough road, the Lt. Colonel Commander saw what I was doing and radioed to his officers that it looked as though I might be successful. "As soon as he's finished," he said, "have the troops leave anything that may drop or fall, sling their rifles over their neck and shoulders and button their steel helmets on tight."

At this point, thinking that we had called in the fighter aircraft, the enemy had begun to pull back, deeper into the woods. Ordinarily, Navy fighter aircraft should have been standing by, taking only a few minutes to get to us, which, in truth, should have been the first command given by our Commanding Officer. But unfortunately, he'd neglected to do, putting our lives in great danger. I've never understood, even to this day, why it wasn't done.

Still in my vehicle, I cautiously drove up to the enemy's booby-trapped truck, well aware that it was set to explode upon contact. After determining that I couldn't get past unless I moved it, I maneuvered slowly up to the loaded 'bomb-on-wheels' and nudged it gently until it rolled off the rocks. I sat there, my heart pounding, watching as it spun slowly, almost silently down a 1200-1500 foot drop off the mountainside. That silence was quickly broken by the deafening sound of the explosion once it hit ground bottom. You could literally feel the earth shaking. My thoughts raced from unimaginable pressure to determination and finally relief.

Putting the truck in reverse, I backed up and drove in a straight line approximately 8-10 yards. I only had about 10 more yards to go when the enemy hurriedly repositioned a machine gun and opened up, shooting down on me from the hilltop. I thought to myself, 'they just might get me here.' But I had no other choice than to go for it.

Luckily, the enemy's guns weren't zeroed and the bullets thankfully went right over me. They then switched to the machine gun and began firing, targeting the trucks loaded with ammunition. Had they been successful, it would have been all over for me. I sped up and cut hard. At that moment, another machine gun opened up right in my ear, but I was too busy driving and holding my machine gun in the firing position to initially notice who it was. I looked up and saw a Lt. Colonel up on the running board. He said, "Drive on Corporal, I've got you covered. I've got those bastards." First thing I thought was, 'Thank God, I'm safe.' After driving another 10 yards, I pulled over to the right and stopped. For about 2 hours, our men came out of that minefield with their hands up in the air. The Lt. Colonel had instructed them to raise both hands to maintain balance and walk in the center of the truck tracks I'd created to be able to make it out of the minefield. One stumble and you would have set them off. Infantry battalion, including rifle companies A, B and C, three tanks and other elements and support troops reinforced the roughly 1,500 men walking out of that minefield. The pride I felt was, and still to this day, is indescribable, knowing that my efforts helped lead these soldiers to safety. I hope and pray that any one of these men who might still be alive today, come forward to help corroborate these accounts as they took place.

The Lt. Colonel obtained all my identifying information and said he was going to have my Company Commander and possibly the Regimental Commander bring me back to this location once the minefields were cleared to see how the 'Man Upstairs' protected me so that I could in turn, save the lives of the others. "I'll see to it that you're taken care of," he said. "You're number one, and I'll make certain that you receive the proper credit. You just do not understand what you've accomplished."

As a soldier on the battlefield, you never do anything with the thought of receiving a commendation for your efforts or bravery. You do it because that's how you're taught and trained to respond to danger. However, after the acknowledgement from the Lt. Colonel, I felt sure that my country would recognize and show gratitude for my extraordinary sacrifice to duty and country. There was and is still, no doubt in my mind that the Commander nominated me for the *Congressional Medal of Honor*. But after years of waiting, hoping and trusting in the integrity of our nation, it never came. I would like to believe that the Lt. Colonel would have kept his word, and don't understand why there was never any mention of a nomination. Perhaps, I've thought, he didn't survive later battles to tell of my heroics. But I do think however that if any of those men that I aided are still alive, they wouldn't hesitate to come forward to uphold the facts as they happened that day.

I do believe that had I received the Congressional Medal of Honor, that instead of being a retired 1st Sergeant, I would have retired as a General. At that rating, I could have returned home and attended the State University with no problem, and still maintained my military schedule. My objective now is to bring my story to the attention of the Commander in Chief of the United States of America.

OLD TRIPLE NICKLES

After the minefield incident, I was transferred to the 159th field artillery in Korea, an all black support unit based in Oklahoma and known as the 'Old Triple Nickles.' The 159th never lost a gun to the enemy, a record few other 105-mm gun battalions could match. They were one of the last segregated all black combat units of the U.S. Army. The original 555th Parachute Infantry Battalion, or "Triple Nickles," succeeded in becoming the nation's first African-American parachute infantry battalion and the first African American unit to be integrated into the "regular" army shortly after World War II.

One day, I happened to be on line and volunteered in support of a black tank unit in retaking Seoul, the Capital of South Korea. One of the greatest leaders this country ever produced in my opinion was General Douglas MacArthur who stopped by to review the line. MacArthur, who understood infantry tactics, had warned the

Chinese that if they entered the fray, he would have no problem dropping the feared Atom bomb, or 'A-bomb' as it was more commonly known, which at that time, was in sole possession by the U.S. He believed the United Nations forces should advance into China to destroy the communist government rather than limit the Korean War to a stalemate. But after the defeat of the North Koreans, the Chinese did intervene. The Chinese entry caused an immediate escalation of the U.S. air campaign. General MacArthur ordered that a wasteland be created between the fighting front and the Chinese border, destroying from the air every installation, factory, city, and village over thousands of square miles of North Korean territory. MacArthur said he had a plan that would have won the war in 10 days: "I would have dropped 30 or so atomic bombs," he told an interviewer in December 1950, "and the war would have ended victoriously for the U.S."

General MacArthur was prepared to give China a deadline for troop withdrawal, and if they refused, I really think we would have launched the bomb. To this day I believe our commander held the best hand. MacArthur, I feel, was a great man and I'm certain there were and still are plenty of soldiers who'd agree. As a soldier, I will always respect both General MacArthur and General George Patton's tactics of once the enemy attacks the only thing he understands is defeat and; never start a battle unless you plan to win.

Once, while on special duty, I was called out from a foxhole and noticed grown men shedding tears. Truman had replaced MacArthur with General Matthew B.

Ridgway. My belief is that if President Truman had left General MacArthur in charge, there would only be one Korea. Ridgeway, who strongly opposed segregation of forces, met strong opposition from Major General Edward M. Almond. Almond would re-segregate already integrated units and deny approval of medals for black soldiers. Still, the 24th Infantry achieved the first victory of the war, after the invasion of Pusan Perimeter in 1950, and the first medals of Honor were awarded to black soldiers from the unit. The victory gained national prestige, shown in newspapers all over the U.S., though not remembered for long. An official Army history of the first six months of the Korean War, *'South to Naktong, North to the Yalu,'* written by Roy Appleman, a civilian historian commissioned to write the history of the 24th, denied that a battle ever took place at Yech'on. "Appleman wrote that the 24th was lousy, an embarrassment to the army and to the American people and labeled the unit as cowards," remembers General Oliver Dillard. According to the General, the enlisted men of the 24th and those who'd served with the unit were devastated to read or hear of this review. "The Chief of Staff hand-picked Colonel John Cash, a black intelligence officer and Vietnam combat leader and one of the highest ranking historians assigned to the Center of Military History to validate or invalidate Appleman's description of the 24th," recalled Dillard. So as a result, in 1989 Cash took Dillard and seven other veterans of the 24th back to Korea to relive those dreadful early days of the war. The trip was an emotional journey, suffused with anger at the Army for its alleged injustice to blacks.

The commander of the 25th Division, Major General William Kean awarded Black officer Charles M. Bussey for his achievements in this battle. Lieutenant Colonel John T. Corley, Regimental Commander of the 24th Infantry Regimental Combat Team of the 25th Infantry Division also firmly upheld the battle at Yech'on.

A GROUND SHAKING EXPERIENCE

After completing my overseas assignment and returning to the U.S., I stopped in Oakland, California. While on base, the Commanding Officer said he wanted to see me in his office. He initially asked how I liked California, and then said he wanted to keep me there for a short time and make me Assistant 1st Sergeant based on my fine combat record and overall qualifications. I couldn't help but wonder if he'd known about the minefield incident in Korea or if he'd felt that I should have been recognized and was deserving of the *Congressional Medal of Honor*. He mentioned that he felt I should have been appointed to a commission, and that he was willing to help me get it. Initially, I considered staying, but then I encountered my first earthquake, then another one. So after just one month, I decided to leave, due in part to my experience back home in Grady when I was about 8-years old.

As a young child, I preferred to be alone rather than

hanging out in the street with the other kids in the neighborhood. I even asked to have my bedroom on the other side of the house, away from my siblings. I did however enjoy hanging around with my dad. There was always something to learn from him. At first, mother was against having my room far away from the others, but I convinced her that it was only because it made me feel as though I had my own little space in a house filled with six girls and six boys.

We had a large, V-shaped radio at the time that stood alone as a beautiful piece of furniture in the living room of our house. It provided us with news, weather, and sports reports for many years. But the radio had recently broken and had yet to be replaced.

On one particular day I noticed thick, darkening clouds outside, an indication that a storm was brewing in the atmosphere. We hadn't heard any reports from anyone of how bad it would be. Now, it was well known that members of my father's family were psychics, but until that night, I hadn't realized that my dad was too. After everyone had gone to bed that evening, dad turned to mother and told her to go into my sister's bedroom and have them move to another bedroom on the other side of the house. Of course they complained of being tired and already settled in their own beds, but dad and mother insisted.

At approximately 3 a.m. the next morning, I heard a noise that sounded like 10 locomotives, and we didn't live anywhere near the railroad. A vicious storm had come over night with strong winds, pounding rain and spouts. In front of our house stood two large trees transplanted from California. The diameter of some of the tree limbs was huge, similar in size to a 50-gallon drum. The storm, with its howling wind and beating rain had picked up the tree nearest to the house and tossed it into the air, landing it onto the roof and into the house. It happened fast, resonating like an explosion, and coming to rest dangerously close to my bed. You could barely get your pinky finger between the limb and the bed railing. In my sister's bedroom, there was nothing left, everything was destroyed. Had they remained there, they would not have survived. Even the new stove and ice chest my dad had just recently purchased were destroyed. I thanked God that he'd had the foresight to recommend moving my sisters to the spare bedroom. I couldn't bear the thought of having lost members of my beloved family.

Although we lived under the harsh laws of segregation, the whites in town always respected the Gibson family. And after the storm, word got out that our house had been partially destroyed. Members of the community, black and white, brought over food, a brand new stove, and a large ice chest after local carpenters had come with lumber and nails, working for hours from morning to nightfall, completely reconstructing our home. This near tragedy only strengthened my faith in God and the kindness of man.

So after experiencing the quakes in Oakland, and remembering that night in Grady, I was more than ready to move on from California.

BACK AT FORT DIX

After leaving Oakland, I was reassigned to Fort Dix, NJ where I worked as an Infantry instructor. My Commanding Officer resembled Lt. Gen. Russel Honore, the retired Lieutenant General who served as the 33rd commanding general of the U.S. First Army at Fort Gillem, Georgia, and commander of Joint Task Force Katrina, responsible for coordinating military relief efforts for the Hurricane Katrina affected areas across the Gulf Coast. I worked there for about a year before requesting another overseas assignment. I was given a choice of Japan or Europe—I chose Europe. I'd already spent enough time in Japan.

THE REUNION

I requested assignment to the Tank Infantry School of the 2nd Armored Division located near the French border, near a town called Baumholder in Germany. I arrived at the Tank Infantry School and was tested and qualified as a Tank Gunnery Instructor. The unit I'd left before volunteering for the job as weapons instructor in Baumholder was the 2nd Armored Division 'C' Company in Straubine, Germany, near Weisboden, the same unit Elvis Presley would join a few months later.

I was able to go to school at night after duties and thoroughly enjoyed my time there. But as it had become custom, after 18 months, I felt it was time to move on.

During that time in Europe, we'd had orders that said you had to stay where you were, you couldn't move or couldn't transfer out. But I'd heard of a unit that guarded the border between Czechoslovakia and Russia and reasoned that they'd have a need for a good, experienced soldier. I'd also made time to always read the army newspapers and publications to keep up with what was happening in and around me and throughout the military. One article in particular caught my eye. It was written about my former commander from back in Japan and Korea, Brigadier General John T. Corley, who served as the Regimental Commander of the 24th Infantry Regimental Combat Team of the 25th Infantry Division. He'd gotten promoted to 2-Star General. I knew he'd remember me as the one to call when someone needed rescuing. Stationed in Stuttgart, Germany at the time, General Corley was G1, in charge of personnel and G2, Intelligence. I went to the military office and asked for a 3-day pass to go to Stuttgart.

Once I arrived in Stuttgart, I immediately went to General Corley's office. I showed my ID to the Major who said, "I know you're a soldier, I can look at you and tell. You don't need to show ID." I asked to see General Corley.

"Do you know him?" he asked. I mustered up a firm, "Yes sir I know him, and all you have to do is ask him if he remembers Sergeant Gibson." The Major offered me a seat and disappeared into the General's office. I could hear their brief conversation. "You're damned right I know him," the General said. "Bring him in here." He'd seemed to have known about everything I'd accomplished in my military career. He said to the Major, "Come. I want you to meet a damn good man." Standing in the door of his office with a look of unbridled pride, he said, "Sergeant Gibson, front and center." I walked in and saluted him. I told him that I'd known he was there and wanted to say hello and explained that I understood his rules of no one transferring out, but with my record, and now feeling it unnecessary to repeat my successes, I told him that I'd wanted to go to the border units where I could get in some action. I also asked for some time off.

"Whatever you want," he answered. "I'll have the Major take care of it and I'll tell the new Commanders what to expect when you arrive. And, Sergeant, if you ever need me for *anything*, just call." He turned and asked, "Can you take care of it Major? If not, I'll put somebody else on it." With a swift nod of understanding, the Major acknowledged his responsibility. "Give him orders before he leaves here," Corley continued, this time looking directly at me. "How much time do you want off, Sergeant Gibson?"

"Ten days will be okay," I answered. He turned to the Major and gave the order. "Give him 15." The best part was that the days weren't chargeable to the mandated 30 days a soldier gets per year.

I used the time off to familiarize myself with Czechoslovakia, to get a feel for how I'd be living, and to see if it would be conducive to what I'd been accustomed. I knew that if I didn't feel comfortable there, I could always just stay where I was near the French border. After meeting some of the people and the Company Commander, I decided that I would indeed accept the assignment.

DANCING THE NIGHT AWAY

To say that I am a gifted dancer is an understatement. I recall one night while I was in Ludwigsburg, near Stuttgart, that I went out to listen to a few German bands and watch the people dance the European Waltz. Another American soldier was there and asked if I even knew how to perform the dance. 'Sure,' I answered and went over to a table to ask a young German woman to dance. She replied, 'Dankeschon,' thank you in German, but inquired quizzically as to whether or not I knew how to dance *their* waltz. Although she didn't quite understand my English response, I ended up taking her around the dance floor more than once. Everyone stood up and applauded my flawless effort! Afterwards, a woman who'd noticed my dancing invited me to a Bavarian party. She told me that there would be more than 4,000 people in attendance. I asked whether there would be any former Nazi's there because at that time, wherever we went, we had to wear our military uniforms. The woman replied, "No, there will be no Nazi's there. Your great General George S. Patton took care of that." I laughed and accepted the invitation. A limousine was sent to take me to the ball where all the beautiful girls stood around the floor, waiting their turn to waltz around the magnificent dance floor with me. I had a memorable time.

OFF TO CZECHOSLOVAKIA

After being assigned to the Huntsfield area near the Czechoslovakian border with the 81st Reconnaissance, I worked as a Patrol Leader. I remember how adept the Russian and Czechoslovakian soldiers were at 'trick tactics.' They were not above using booby-trapped dogs with explosives strapped to their backs. The dogs were trained to not bark, but to run under U.S. and allied vehicles and set off the explosives. This maneuver kept you alert for anything approaching your location, ready to react immediately to any situation. There was a situation one night at an outpost when troops opened up immediately on a charging dog who was seconds away from setting off deadly explosives.

Because the border wasn't clearly marked in many areas, you really had to know how to read and understand maps to know where you were at all times. I happened to be good with maps and one of the few non-commissioned officers qualified to lead a border patrol.

Once I lead a patrol with a getaway vehicle, and three fighting vehicles. The enemy had brought out about 200 infantry, which I'm pretty sure I could have taken out with my 50-caliber machine gun. I was forward facing them. The 2nd jeep was in a partial defilade position, using natural or artificial obstacles to conceal its whereabouts. The jeep had its 3.5mm rocket launcher turned on the enemy tank. The 3rd jeep, the get-away jeep was almost 3 miles to the rear and never stopped moving, slowly forward or backward. With my unit's immediate show of force, the enemy withdrew. I ordered all three vehicles to stand down and return to normal patrol. There were numerous volatile situations like this and any wrong move could have started another war.

In another precarious situation, I noticed a lady and man walking across a field, not far from the border crossing. Not knowing if they were aware of their position, I got on the radio and said, 'attention all jigsaw [sic] stations, I'm monitoring an incident which could lead to something. I'm checking it out. After just a short while, I said, 'You're in 'Bravo Situation now.'

Forty miles back was a base camp where the Company commander monitored the radio all the time. He'd heard me say I was going down to check things out. I wanted to get between the civilians and the border because of their close proximity to it. I took off toward the border and gave the order to execute my precise commands.

As I moved out, the enemy pulled out a Stalin tank. One of my fighting vehicles went straight past me in a partial defilade position where it would have been hard for the enemy to bring direct fire on him. I yelled, 'Bravo situation, Bravo situation,' indicating that all vehicles should get in position. The jeeps took off, even those carrying rocket launchers, and went right near a bridge in a partial defilade position. Once in position, they all reported: 'Team leader, in position, in position, got you covered.' The jeep that would take care of the Stalin tank was in position first, reporting in. I was still exposed, but once I approached the man and lady, I explained to them that they were in danger near the Czechoslovakian and Russian Border. Well, I think the man took off running faster than the woman! They had been visiting someone in the area and were unaware of how close to peril they'd come. We brought out the troops and the tanks followed.

I received a call from the base station Commander giving a call sign to inform me that he'd scrambled the jets for additional cover. Twelve tanks began moving into position. There were about 20 Czechoslovakians heading for the border. Within seconds, the American fighter jets were circling overhead, listening for any and all communication. At the all clear, they dipped their wings as a gesture of salutation. I saluted them, and contacting my base station Commander, said that there was no need to scramble the jets any further, everything was under control. The enemy was no longer a threat. My Commanding Officer radioed: "You may break contact. I'll do the same." He halted his tanks and returned to base. I received outstanding commendations for my handling of the overall situation.

FORT POLK - LOUISIANNA

After completing a 3-year tour of duty in Europe, I was called to personnel and asked where I'd like to be stationed within the United States. I requested Fort Dix, NJ again, choosing to be close to home. But, I'd said, if that wasn't available, I'd settle for any base located in the north. I was shipped to Fort Polk, Louisiana, as far south as your could go. The Ku Klux Klan would come on base and set fire to their crosses of hate. At that time, Fort Polk was the only military base in the army without a club facility for socializing. There was only a little shed, with no walls. You could purchase beer there. About five miles off base, near Leesville, Louisiana, there was a small facility known as the 'service club' with two pool tables inside.

Once you left the base and reached the outside road, you could go straight, left or right. A large sign that read: *Entire area off limits to all of African descent* awaited departing soldiers. State troopers sat outside the gate of the base. If you were African-American and left base, *and* had out of state license plates, like my New Jersey plates, the trooper or troopers would pull you over for a random check, look inside your car or trunk for anything they deemed illegal that could possibly send you off to jail.

I recall one incident when I went out with a couple of guys from the base to a club in town. I always wore my uniform. One of the guys, who looked to weigh almost 200 pounds, decided to wear civic clothing. The club was set up like an old tobacco storage house, long and narrow, with very few room dividers. It had been used previously just that purpose. The club proprietor, Mr. Crank, greeted us in his converted nightclub and expressed his gratitude for our service to country.

I always sat up front wherever I went so that I'd be able to watch everything around me. There were plenty of beautiful women in the club that evening, many of whom looked to be of Creole decent. They were dressed nicely. But most of the men were dressed shoddily. The guys and I definitely stood out.

One of the men I was with, Corporal Neil from South Carolina, offered to get the first round of drinks. I asked for a large soda. The bar was located towards the back of the club. As Neil walked down the aisle towards the bar, I noticed one of the locals brandishing a knife. I alerted Neil who immediately picked up a chair and knocked the knife out of the guy's hand. Another man came in looking for trouble. I knew I needed to take him out. He said, "Don't you move sir. I know you're an officer, but I have a gun and I won't hesitate to kill you with it."

I immediately called upon my skills and training in Karate, all the while psychologically degrading the pistol packing hoodlum. Caught off guard, he began shouting, "Get back now, get back. I don't really want to kill you." I told him that if he took a shot at me, he'd better hit his target the first time, because if not, that would be the end of his life. I said, "I'm gonna give you a vacation to hell, 'cause there's no way you're gonna get to Heaven."

By now, the women were screaming, running and jumping out of windows. The first guy to follow them out of the window was the big 200 pounder! Meanwhile, I kept talking trash to the guy in my face, telling him that I would kill him slowly, have him calling out for his mother. I kept my left shoulder in his face to keep him moving for the rear door.

There was one woman left in the club, hiding behind the front door. As I backed the nervous gunman into the door, the woman screamed, startling him, causing his gun to go off. I took him down, knocking the door off its hinges in the melee and watching as he stumbled right through the open doorway. That was quite a night. I held on to a piece of his shirt and gave the gun to Mr. Crank. After being assured that everything was alright I left for base. That was the first and last time I went off base for the weekend.

I was made Assistant 1st Sergeant at base camp, but ended up more or less doing the Lieutenants' work. Assignments ranged from maintaining troop information, to building inspections. I was the highest-ranking minority at Fort Polk. Even so, it seemed the racist were always out to get me. On one occasion, before a building inspection, a few soldiers snuck inside the quarters near someone's bed and poured paint all over the floor. I quickly cleaned it up before inspection. This happened on more than just one occasion, so I knew it was done deliberately.

Things got so bad and out of hand at Fort Polk that I looked for somewhere else to go, anywhere else but here. After reading the Army Time Stars and Stripes cover to cover, I noticed a recruitment ad for Airborne Rangers. Even with my combat experience, I knew I'd met all the criteria, but I also knew that if I'd apply directly, they'd more than likely just laugh at me. I needed help from someone with power and influence. I wrote to Representative James Auchincloss, my Congressional Representative back home in Middlesex County, New Jersey and referred him to the ad in the Army newspaper. I asked if he'd spearhead my request. Mr. Auchincloss replied immediately, telling me that he'd assist in any way he could.

I was comforted knowing that hopefully my time at Fort Polk would end soon. But before any of that came to be, another incident happened where one kid from Arkansas and another from one of the Carolinas, both admitted racists, talked about me disparagingly to anyone who'd listen. However, when it came time for me to move on, my Commander, looking over the list I'd prepared of who should advance, noticed the very two names who'd spread the hateful lies. He said, "Are you sure you want to promote *all* these people?" I said, 'Yes sir. There's a couple over there that are question marks, but this will probably help them understand the new world that's unfolding before their eyes.' He said he understood where I was coming from and signed off on the list.

One evening, before I'd left, both young men knocked on the door of my quarters. I gave them permission to enter and offered them folding chairs to sit on. They declined, saying that they were not worthy to sit on the chairs, and with my permission, would rather sit on the floor. I told them to make themselves comfortable. Before long, they were crying like babies. 'What's the problem?' I asked. They said they'd come there to ask my forgiveness and confessed that they'd tried to do everything to make my time at Fort Polk miserable. "Where we come from," one confessed, "we're taught not to care about or respect black people or their rank, or education." The second man finished by declaring, "We were always told that blacks were good for nothing." Both acknowledged that even though they'd said and done everything to distract me from my duties and had tried on numerous occasions to get me in trouble with the superior officers, I still promoted them. The only thing they felt could be done now was to beg my forgiveness. I did forgive them and later told the Commander that I felt those two would end up being good soldiers who would ultimately realize that once bullets started to fly, a man's color shouldn't mean a thing.

Representative Auchincloss wrote back and advised me to consult with a doctor to make sure I was in top physical condition for the training I would undertake as an Airborne Ranger. Although I knew I was already in good shape, I was determined to be in even better physical condition.

The doctor recommended a healthy eating regimen and an even stricter workout routine. After daily duty, I would run for 2 miles every day and eventually worked my way up to more than twenty miles a day, running almost 4 hours a day. The Congressman and a black non-commissioned officer recommended that I retake the entire battery of tests. I did, and improved my battery score. I laugh now when I think back on the last words the post Commander at Fort Polk said to me once he became aware that I was leaving. "You're the highest rankingest Negri we ever had down here," he muttered in a long southern drawl. "Why do you want to leave? We have some pretty girls down here." I told him I was aware of all that, but wanted to be closer to home. Fort Polk was an eye opening experience in race relations in 1950s America.

FORT CAMPBELL KENTUCKY - AIRBORNE

Before leaving Fort Polk, I noticed on both sides of my army record jacket folder, there was a large red letter 'P' that stood for 'Political Influence.' It didn't matter to me at the time because I was happy to get out of what I'd considered not much more than a 'hell hole.'

Fort Campbell is proud to be the home of the only Air Assault Division in the world, the 101st Airborne Division. After reporting to Fort Campbell in 1958, one of the only bases sitting in two states, Kentucky and Tennessee, I was instructed to report to the amphitheater where I found a seat near the back among 316 other personnel. The Platoon leader got up to speak, beginning his speech by saying, "Once you qualify as Airborne, you can easily defeat any 5 non-airborne soldiers. This is what we teach and this is what we believe. If ever a non-airborne soldier opposes you after you've successfully completed this training, there's no doubt who'll win. And one more thing," he said in a voice resonant with sternness, "We *despise* politicians. Sergeant Gibson, front and center!" I snapped to attention and made my way down to the Platoon leader as fast as my legs allowed. "When we ask for 10 pushups," he bellowed, looking straight at me, "we're talking about airborne pushups. You might do 100 regular push-ups just *trying* to do 10 airborne pushups." I dropped down and knocked em' out with barely a noticeable sweat. I was in shape and ready for anything they'd throw at me. "Recover, recover," the Platoon leader shouted, glancing toward the other officers and shaking his head. In just those few moments, I had proven myself. I felt untouchable.

After a short while, all 317 of us were dismissed to begin training. Initially, you were required to run, not jog, for at least three miles. The men seemed to be in decent shape, but I found them all following behind me.

In an attempt to express how much they resented me being there because of the help I'd received from Representative Auchincloss, the training officers did everything in their power to make me quit. During one training session, the instructor waited until I was near a large patch of frozen ice and made me drop, right there, on the ice, and do 100 pushups. I managed to push them out even though I was extremely cold. By doing at least 600-700 pushups a day on my own, helped my stamina and endurance and kept me in top physical condition. I would need to call upon this disciplined mind-set during airborne training.

I can't say for sure whether or not the training officers were prejudiced, because there was a white soldier from Oklahoma who said they were also riding him to quit—not by doing unbearable pushups, but by using other harsh tactics. He vowed he would try to stick it out. "Well, if you're in shape," I said, "they can't defeat you. But if you feel you're unable to carry on, you may as well go and tell 'em that you're ready to resign right now." I told him it was my belief that if you commit to doing something, just do it. He agreed with me. But in the end, he ended up quitting.

On the day of graduation, all personnel were required to run 5 miles on what seemed to be an extraordinarily cold day. The instructor pulled me out of the formation and directed me to knock out at least 100 *airborne pushups*. He kept telling me to move over, until finally, I found myself in a ditch with my right hand cut from a broken piece of glass. The blood flowed freely from my hand, but I ignored it. I didn't want to give him the satisfaction of knowing that I was injured in any way. The Instructor shouted, "218, (my military number) why don't you quit." I told him he didn't have enough guts to make me quit. "And don't try catching up with the others when you're done," he continued, "Just head back." "No," I said, "I'll catch up." I had about a half mile to go in a dead run. I then turned to the instructor and shouted, "You can follow me and I'll make *you* quit."

"Get the hell out of here," he yelled, flabbergasted at failed attempt at making me give up. Out of the class of 317 personnel, of which 93 graduated, I finished first. I came in at *number one*.

While the Commander reviewed the graduates, a

FORT CAMPBELL KENTUCKY - AIRBORNE

Hispanic guy walked near me and said, "I'm damn proud of you. Everybody knows about you." I didn't recognize him, couldn't place his face and wasn't sure if he was one of the instructors. I could only speculate that he was referring to the minefield incident. The Commanding Officer, who we referred to as the Japanese leader, Hideki Tojo, because of his bald head, was stopped by the Commanding General of the Jump School and said, "Although I have somewhere else to go, I just want to meet that damn Sergeant Gibson."

"Sergeant Gibson, on the double, front and center," the Commanding Officer yelled out. I snapped to attention and saluted the Commanding General. He shook my hand and said, "I just wanted to meet you. I figured you'd had combat experience. You've made asses out of all of them." I smiled slightly, but on the inside I was damn near laughing. He wished me well and continued on to his next appointment.

THE JUMP MASTER

Still determined to make me quit—even after graduation, three instructors had been assigned the task. To qualify as an Airborne Ranger, you were required to make five or six jumps from a 30-foot tower. I must have made 80 jumps. You were also required to put on a dummy bag filled with about 40 pounds of sand to simulate the weight of a parachute. I'm almost certain my chute had 50 or more pounds in the bag and you had to do squat jumps until you were called.

With interlocked fingers over my steel helmet, the orders were to jump and bounce until told to come up. I would complete the jumps with aching, numb muscles and plenty of determination. There were a few guys who sustained broken ankles, legs and even broken backs from jumping out of the towers.

When it came time to making the first parachute jump, the Jump Master would go through the jump commands. With about five minutes to go after crossing

THE JUMP MASTER

Highway 41A, which runs from Paducah, Kentucky to Nashville, Tennessee, our marking area for making the jumps, the Jump Master yelled, "Drop zone coming up. Sergeant Gibson, stand in the door." We were jumping at 1,000 feet. "What if the main chute doesn't open?" he asked. 'I'll open the second parachute,' I responded. He continued, seemingly trying to unnerve me. "What if *that* chute doesn't open?" he asked with a visible smirk. 'I personally don't give a damn,' I answered, and jumped straight out the door. There were no more comments from him that day.

SERGEANT GIBSON IN PARACHUTE JUMP SUIT

101ST AIRBORNE DIVISION AND THE KU KLUX KLAN

After completing the Airborne Ranger course, I was assigned to the Reconnaissance Unit of the 101st Airborne Division. General Westmoreland, a fine officer, was the Commander General of the entire 101st Airborne Division at that time. But there was always that one guy in the group ready and willing to cause trouble. This particular soldier liked shooting pool with everybody while bragging that he was a card-carrying member of the Ku Klux Klan (KKK), a clear violation of army regulation. I was in charge of the Reconnaissance Platoon—the eyes and ears of the 101st Airborne Division. It had been decided that because of my combat experience, I would share responsibilities as commander with the card carrying KKK soldier.

"Look here," I'd cautioned him, "You're a soldier in uniform. I don't care how you feel about your KKK membership or how you feel about minorities, you're an

American first, and you don't brag about what you consider your personal exploits around the troops."

Often socializing with people he outranked, this soldier would unexpectedly and unprovoked, especially when full of beer, pick up an object and hit someone in the head with it, causing an injury severe enough to land them in the hospital. I remember saying to him, "Now, there are 43 of us in the Recon Unit, and the next time I hear that you've caused someone to land in the hospital, I'm gonna get you. I won't necessarily kill you, but I'm gonna put something on you that'll make you wish you were dead. So, I'm making it very clear to you Sergeant, right now it's a warning, later on it'll be a threat."

With a look of extreme annoyance over his face, he replied, "Well it looks like me and you are just gonna have to have it out."

"Yep," I said with stealth confidence. "You and I sure are gonna have it out and guess what brother, you're gonna lose every time." One day, I gave him a good lesson by locking him inside his own office. Once I'd decided to let him out, I had to physically restrain him before he could grab a tire rod that sat behind his desk. I think he knew from that day who was the stronger man.

Most Fridays, we'd move out with combat equipment and board an aircraft at approximately 3 a.m. flying around the area near Fort Campbell, then return and drop about 40-50 miles from base conducting war games. The Lieutenant in charge of the platoon said to me, "Sergeant Gibson, you'll take the lead and the guy that gets back first will have a day off."

Now my nickname in the 101st and the 82nd Airborne

had been the 'horseman' because of my endurance, and I was not about to relinquish that title to a self-described bigot.

We'd split the personnel in half. I'd take twenty and leave the other twenty for him. I'd lay out the map and a compass and plot a direct route back to base. Sometimes there would be water in the way. But if it didn't look too deep or too threatening, I'd take a stick, measure it, and then take the shortest man in the platoon and put him behind me. I'd tell the men that no matter what happened, if someone fell, they had to wait, never leave him there alone. Once we entered the water, the person behind me would hold onto my belt with his right hand. This was done with precision all the way back to the tallest Ranger in the rear to make sure that everyone remained safe and intact. My team made it back first that time and most times afterwards.

UNEXPECTED DISCOVERY

I recall once having to use my dagger to chop thick brush filled with small Brazilian trees when all of a sudden, I came to an open space with about six small Evergreen trees. I could tell that a house had been there at one time. I looked around. Through the clearing I found a small monument with a metal piece on a stone face. The inscription read: *Homestead of the great Edgar Cayce, the Sleeping Prophet.* Cayce was the most documented psychic of the 20th century. I'd read most of his books and believed in most of his theories. For forty-three years of his adult life, Edgar Cayce demonstrated the uncanny ability to put himself into a kind of self-induced sleep state by lying down on a couch, closing his eyes, and folding his hands over his stomach. This state of relaxation and meditation enabled him to place his mind in contact with all time and space. From this state he could respond to questions as diverse as: *What are the secrets of the universe?* to *How can I remove a stubborn wart?* His responses to these questions came to be called, 'readings' and contain insights so valuable, that even to this day, individuals have found practical help for everything from maintaining a well-balanced diet and improving human relationships, to overcoming life-threatening illnesses and experiencing a closer walk with God.

ARKANSAS SEGREGATION

During the time of segregation, Arkansas stood steadfast in their belief that blacks and whites should continue to be separated in every facet of life, except when blacks were employed by whites as housemaids, janitors, or some other laborious position.

The Little Rock Nine were a group of African-American students who were enrolled in Little Rock Central High School in September 1957 as a result of The U.S. Supreme Court's ruling in the historic Brown v. Board of Education case.

The Governor of Arkansas, Orval Faubus, in opposition to the Court's ruling, activated and deployed the Arkansas National Guard to support the segregationists in early September of that year. The sight of a line of soldiers blocking nine black students from attending high school immediately polarized the city.

Attorneys from the U.S. Justice Department requested an injunction against the governor's deployment of the

National Guard and Judge Ronald Davies granted the injunction and ordered the governor to withdraw the Guard less than three weeks later.

The 101st Airborne Battle Group, 327th Infantry were ordered to Little Rock by President Eisenhower to enforce the court injunction during the crisis until Thanksgiving when Task Force 153rd Infantry assumed responsibility.

I was with G2 Intelligence and working again for Bradley Biggs. I was responsible for planning during the time of the Arkansas desegregation project. We didn't want to upset the situation anymore than it already was. So when we sent the black soldiers in, we sent them in at night to a gymnasium until any fighting broke out. Only then did the soldiers come out in wedge formation, which is used when the situation is vague or contact is possible, taking an entire street to contain the melee.

IRAN

I served in Iran with the Advisory Group for almost a year. I was stationed in Razi, Tehran, which, according to the Bible, a prophet who did not make it to witness the birth of Christ because he was killed during a series of earthquakes is buried. My duties were to advise and train the Iranian army, teaching them American tactics in Infantry and Artillery. I remember one time being out among the people when one man approached me, speaking politely. I asked him if he knew about Joe Lewis, the famous American boxer. He immediately started boxing. Then I mentioned the word 'Cadillac' and he motioned steering a wheel. I found the Iranians friendly during that time. They seemed to admire Americans.

NORTH CAROLINA AGRICULTURAL & TECHNICAL (A&T) - 1962

Still wanting to complete my education, I took a few courses on base that were offered by the University of North Carolina in general psychology and intelligence. But in order to earn a college degree, I applied at North Carolina Agricultural & Technical (A&T) College located in Greensboro, N.C. in 1962 where the President of the college was the infamous, Dr. Samuel Proctor who served as President/Chancellor from 1960-1964. The retired Major. Gen. Charles D. Bussey, ground commander during the invasion of the 'Pusan Perimeter,' at the town of Yech'on, in 1950, was also a distinguished alumnus of A&T.

The professor of Military Science on base was an African-American who was later promoted from Major to Light Colonel. I went to his office dressed military sharp, like all Airborne, and found him sitting stoically behind his desk. I needed a letter from the Major to be able to attend classes. He looked up and said, without any provocation from me, "I don't like you. You think you're better than us." I was shocked before replying, "Excuse me sir? I have civilian clothes with me. I won't wear a uniform if it causes trouble. I can easily change into civic clothing. I've only come to take courses to try and obtain a college degree." He said, "I'm not even going to talk about that. Now get out of my office." I was stunned. I wondered what I'd done to elicit this type of response. I went back to speak with the Executive Assistant to the Major in the Military Reserve Officer Training Program to try to get an explanation. He was from Alabama and invited me to step into his office. Once inside, I snapped to attention. He saluted me and said, "No, let me salute you. You are a bad motor scooter. I've heard about you." I didn't know what he was referring to until he told me that he'd heard about my accomplishment from white officers, which by now, was about seven years after the time I would have been awarded the Congressional Medal of Honor. I told him that I was just a God fearing soldier who did what he was commanded to do and that God was obviously with me during that time. He tried to assure me that the Major would change his mind regarding attending the classes.

Eventually, he did and decided I should take law courses to sharpen my presentation skills. I didn't understand his reasoning, but like a true soldier, I did what I was assigned to do. I met with a lawyer at the university who calmed my fears and gave me recommendations of how to get started. He told me that he would work with me and offered several books to read. To my surprise, I ended up teaching a class to the student body. The Major invited the college President, Dr. Samuel Proctor down to observe me. Dr. Proctor congratulated me later and said, "Listen, if you ever decide to become a minister, you'd definitely qualify." I believe the Major initially had me teach the law class hoping that I'd fail. But because of Dr. Proctor's enthusiastic response, he backed away from his plan. I accepted the challenge and came out on top.

A three stripe Sergeant who boasted that he was a distant cousin of Louis Jordan, a pioneering American jazz, rhythm & blues musician from the late 1930s to the early 1950s came to my quarters one evening with a proposition he said was from the Major, who was his superior. He asked me to sign a lease to a rather large house. I looked over the documents while he stood there and realized that what he wanted me to do was to manage a house of ill repute, a 'cat house' in return for being able to attend classes. He also said there would be a stipend included for my troubles. I was infuriated and later went down to Atlanta to the Military Inspector General and made a report. After informing the office of what I thought was inappropriate behavior for a service member, I told them I'd decided to return to the 82nd Airborne Division because the assignment I'd requested in the Special Forces as a Green Beret before I went to college had come through.

REAPING WHAT YOU SOW

Prior to joining the Green Beret, I decided to go back home to New Jersey. I used to love to go to Newark to eat and shop. One day while shopping downtown on Broadway, I almost bumped into the Major from North Carolina A&T. I don't recall if any words were spoken between us. I'd told the Captain before I'd left that I was going to the Inspector General's office to tell everything that had happened while I was at North Carolina A&T. I found out later that the Major, who had more than 20 years invested in the military, was given the option to resign or be demoted and possibly court marshaled. The U.S. Army has a policy: "The Commander is responsible for everything his troops do or fail to do."

THE GREEN BERET-
THE 6TH SPECIAL FORCES /
FORT BRAGG, NC

During a visit to Fort Bragg in 1961, President John F. Kennedy sent word to the Special Warfare Center commander, Brigadier General William P. Yarborough, for all Special Forces soldiers to wear their green berets for the event. President Kennedy felt that since they had a special mission, Special Forces should have something to set them apart from the rest. *'The green beret is a symbol of excellence, a badge of courage, a mark of distinction in the fight for freedom.'*

I worked for a guy from upstate New York who I respected very much. He called one day and told me that the General requested that I go and work for him, because I was the highest-ranking SFC E-6 in the U.S. army. He also offered to do what he could to get me promoted. I told him of the trouble I'd had in getting what I felt was a well-deserved advancement and asked if he thought he could get around the Sergeant who was a well-known member of the local KKK, and who would do whatever he could to keep me from rising in the ranks. He urged me to go and take over Headquarter Company for unit inspection duties and assured me with that exposure, if I pulled off a successful inspection, qualifying for a promotion shouldn't be an arduous task. I requested at least two clerks, someone who knew how to type and someone who was trained in basic administration.

> **WHY YOU SHOULD KNOW ABOUT SPECIAL WARFARE**
>
> WE need a greater ability to deal with guerrilla forces, insurrection, and subversion . . . We must be ready now to deal with any size of force, including small externally supported bands of men; and we must help train local forces to be equally effective.
>
> President John F. Kennedy
> Message to Congress, 1961

FROM SPECIAL WARFARE

After only 3 weeks on the job, Headquarters Company was the first to be called for inspection. After the inspectors came through, Headquarter Company was listed as the highest company on the list passing inspection. We maxed out on everything. Because I'd played such an integral part in bringing Headquarters Company up to standard, a suggestion was sent to Headquarters personnel that I be promoted to 1st Sergeant, E-7. The racist Sergeant, I was told, jumped to his feet and said, "Ain't no black going to be promoted to E-7." The story goes that because of his irrational and incessant rants, my superior eventually turned to him and delivered a mighty punch. I was eventually promoted to E-7.

Training for the 6th Special Forces Group was 18 months long at Fort Bragg. There had been other African-Americans in the Green Beret prior to my joining. Those distinguished men were primarily medics. I was set up for the Ranger Course, specializing in weapons and intelligence—the only minority in a class of 360 people. The 2nd Lieutenant told me that training would be hell, but that he had confidence that I'd make it. The Ranger Course was a three week, 256-mile course. We would conduct war games in woods so thick you couldn't tell whether it was day or night. The civilian population in the area was never aware that we were ever there. We'd go in at 1:00 o'clock in the afternoon and take our first break at 1:00 the next morning. There were snake dangers among other threats as we went into undercover areas, sending out reconnaissance patrols.

The Sergeant Major called me out daily to recon an area for enemy activity. It was a six-mile walk away. Everyone else was had been allowed to sleep. Unknowingly, this was a preview as to what I would endure throughout the course. Only one other person that I was aware of endured this type of treatment. The Sergeant Major would refuse to let any other personnel go along with me on these 'special recon' missions, hoping that I'd get lost and make a grave mistake. But out of the 360 people there, I, along with the 2nd Lieutenant were the only ones who never had to go to the hospital because of blistered feet. We were able to carry on just as if it were a mission in Vietnam. After that training course, and after being made aware of a need for a 1st Sergeant, I was asked to take the job, which of course, I accepted. I was responsible for the cadre and the incoming personnel.

I'd taught a course in preparation for safe landings after para jumping in different venues, including water landings. For example, if you are landing in water, you'll want to take precautions, no matter how shallow or deep. You also wouldn't want to panic if your parachute covers you, even though you wouldn't be able to see right away. There was a fine Sergeant who landed in shallow water and drowned, solely because he'd panicked after his chute obstructed his sight.

I also remember conducting an airborne operation near Morgantown, West Virginia where I told everybody that if they saw a mountain as they left the aircraft, not to panic. "It will look as though you're going to hit it, but you're not," I explained. "And you don't want to land in a way that you'll fall and break your bones," I instructed. I then explained the proper way to fall: 'Once you exit the aircraft, immediately start sliding by pulling on the riser strings from the chute. If you want to move to the rear, pull on the risers on the right.'

In the 82nd Airborne, there was a rough-looking Captain of Italian descent who told me that he'd heard I'd been given the nickname, 'the horseman.'

"I have here with me more than 200 people and 2 rifle companies. All of us could end up in Vietnam soon," he said. "I'd like to have somebody here with me that knows how to maneuver the course—someone who could even give *me* some pointers so that I'd be certain that we'll all get what we're supposed to get from this tough course."

I assured him that if he were to give me operation

responsibility, that I'd shut it down within 4-6 hours. He gave me permission to proceed. We boarded the helicopter and within 4½ hours the operation was shut down. A big red smoke bomb, weighing about 2 gallons dropped from the helicopter simulating a live bomb. Now, when the bomb hits you, you want to get out of the area. But I already knew where everyone was or would go. I knew this because of the many bogus patrols I'd been sent on in the area. I asked the Captain how long he wanted me to continue with the exercise and he answered, "Hell, you can do as you please. Do it until you want to end it." I took the map and bombed an entire area and you could see the soldiers running out from their hiding places where they would go to try and get some sleep. I did this for a few areas. I also staked the guys out, 300-400 people. I shut that down in just a few hours. Afterwards, I requested a few non-chargeable days to my yearly leave. During my time off, I went home to New Jersey to visit my parents, who were living with my siblings at this time.

After that experience, the Commanding General, Joseph Warren Stilwell, Jr. requested my services. He had a special assignment in store for me. I truly felt that had he been briefed of my record of accomplishments, the Congressional Medal of Honor would have been awarded.

As one of the few non-commissioned officers that ever held down Colonel assignments, the General told me that I was going to be on a list very few enlisted men find themselves on. "I'm putting you in a Major's slot. I'm putting you in charge of the language school." I'd learned that the Major who was previously in charge of the school had been fired because of his involvement in selling classified information. However, I was never briefed of the specific charges or of his ultimate punishment. I stayed at the language school until I shipped off to Vietnam in 1963.

HURT IN VIETNAM/ DEFECTIVE CHUTES

I was initially stationed in Saigon, but after moving up, I was charged with setting up security in Nha Trang. I quickly applied for warrant commission after arriving there in 1963. I'd received a letter from the Commanding General congratulating me on the test score I'd made, the third highest score during the Vietnam era. He assured me I'd have no problem converting over to a regular commission. I wasn't.

My unit had gone to Song Mao to jump, and as usual, I was on my guard, looking for anything suspicious. The parachutes issued were supposedly new and were already on board the plane. But once I jumped, I knew the chute was defective. I checked it thoroughly after recovering from the accident and found that it was indeed a WWII packed chute—dried out and rotted. I knew that normally when a T-10 parachute opens, you'd feel a jerking motion. However, not this time, I knew something was wrong. I heard an unusual noise. It partially opened, then began breaking apart. I could actually feel the chute literally coming apart. I now know that it was an old WWII T-7 issued parachute. Immediately, I went into a proper parachute-landing fall: my feet together, head straight and facing forward—not looking down, with knees unlocked. This is done automatically, without even thinking about it. You should be relaxed and go with the fall. The first thing hitting the ground would be the ball of your toes. You'd use your thigh muscles to push you up, as well as your upper shoulders. This 'fall design' is to relieve the pressure off the bones so they don't break. I've fallen much further than I fell that time, however, with the chute breaking apart, and surviving, it caused greater injuries than I'd ever experienced in the past.

When jumping from a plane, there's a feeling that you're stationary, and the ground is coming towards you. It only takes 100 feet to kill you. When I made contact with the earth during the parachute jump, I could tell I was hurt. I was semi-conscience. But because I was so close to the ground, everyone thought I'd been hit by the gunfire and a gunship came to my rescue, firing protective fire. They asked, "Gibson, are you still with us?" I answered "yes, but I'm hurt." They hurried me to the first aid area and said they would rush me back to the hospital in Saigon.

There were about 18-20 people on board the helicopter with me. After landing, all of them were taken off the copter before I could even stand up. I thanked God I was still alive. After being x-rayed, I was given the option of being sent to a hospital in the Philippines or back to the

U.S. But since I only had less than 3 months left before my time would have been over anyway, I said I would attempt to tough it out there, in Vietnam. I was never told the real extent of my injuries. In order to speed along my recuperation, I developed a morning regimen of sit-ups until I got to where I could walk without excruciating pain. I didn't request nor accept any rides from anyone. I preferred to walk wherever I needed to go. In my mind, I felt this would help the healing process, all the while strengthening my body. Years later, after suffering different maladies from those injuries, I wrote to the Department of Army in Missouri, a storage unit where military personnel records were kept, trying to get hold of my records and medical reports, but to no avail.

I would still go out and haul formation, but once on my feet for an hour or so, I would go to the clerk's office and say to him, "you know the drill, right?" I had been going to his office for some time now, closing the door, locking it behind me, and lying down on the bare wooden floor to get relief. As time passed, my injuries had not healed as I'd expected. I went to Ft. Bragg's Hospital and told them I felt constant pain in my left kidney area. I knew something was wrong. But the results of my x-rays, I was told, were normal.

THE OLD GULF WAR

I was ordered to Active duty in March of 1991 for Desert Storm, but the war ended before I deployed.. I received a letter that said in essence, I'd served honorably and that if my experience were required they would like to know if I would join up again. I of course, once again said that I would be happy to join. I headed down to Fort Mead, Maryland and was surprised to learn that the news media in Maryland wanted to interview me for my prior military accomplishments.

A few white men knocked on my door one day and said they wanted to meet me because, they said, they understood that I was one of the highest decorated persons down there. I graciously thanked them, even though I hadn't told anyone of my awards or decorations.

Later, I received a letter from the Commander of the Gulf War requesting a list of all my awards and decorations. I think this was because he'd known that I'd mentioned to the Sergeant Major that the Congressional

Medal of Honor was missing from the list.

We were informed that we could be called for duty overseas. In the meantime, we'd be engaged in support activities. I was given a job working alongside a man named Chris Williams who dealt with ammunition. I went to work as his right-hand man. During one particular week, he invited me to the Baltimore Sea Harbor fest. "You won't have to spend any money," he said, "but if you want to bring something back, it'll cost little or nothing." I accepted his invitation and agreed to meet him after church services one Sunday.

I recall that particular day because the temperature rose to 102 degrees and the air conditioning system at Reverend Pitman's church went out. Reverend Pitman was originally from Mississippi. The pastor suggested to the men in the congregation that if they wanted to remove their suit jackets, they could do so. He assured everyone that he would continue his sermon despite the sweltering heat, but they'd be forgiven if they wanted to leave.

The Reverend ran a bit over his usual sermon length, perhaps drained from the oppressive heat, but I remained seated right where I was, uncomfortable, however willing to suffer a bit longer to hear God's words. After the service, I went to my car and headed towards Chris' home. His wife, who noticed me as I pulled up in the driveway and got out of my car, rushed to the door. "My goodness," she said. "Didn't you see Chris?"

"No," I answered. "Well you should have seen him as he passed down the road," she explained. "He waited around for you and finally figured you weren't coming.

So he left for the Sea Harbor fest."

I must have looked hot and dehydrated because she offered me a cool drink. I thanked her for her hospitality, but graciously declined and went back to base. Once I'd returned, I entered the cool building and immediately felt the urge to urinate. I went into a bathroom stall and had the normal feeling of urination, when in reality I was passing blood, streaming down into the urinal. I was shocked!

I quickly gathered my thoughts and cleaned myself. I hurriedly walked out of the bathroom and upstairs and down the hallway to the apartment of a fellow soldier. I knocked on his door and said to him, "Listen, I need to make a call. I think I need to get to Walter Reed Medical Center in D.C. as fast as I can." Walter Reed was approximately 25 miles away. After making the call to Walter Reed and informing them that I'd felt my left kidney was causing the pain from the injury I sustained in Vietnam, I was advised to go to the Fort Mead Medical Center to be immediately transported by ambulance to their facility in Bethesda. As I entered the Fort Mead Medical Center, there was a long line of military wives waiting to be seen by medical personnel. I calmly explained my urgent need to cut to the front of the line.

I was able to see a nurse right away and shared with her the conversation I'd had with the folks at Walter Reed and their instructions to have me transported immediately by ambulance. The nurse explained that she couldn't authorize anything before the doctor examined me. I then told her I felt as though I'd already lost a quart of blood and felt lightheaded and dizzy. She immediately called for the doctor.

Once the doctor arrived in the examination room, she requested a cup of urine for testing. I told her that I couldn't urinate. The nurse explained to the doctor what I'd told her about passing blood.

The doctor conferred with the nurse and informed her that she couldn't send me over to Walter Reed because of bed shortages. Although I was in pain, I tried to explain that it was Walter Reed Hospital who'd initially made the request. The doctor turned around and walked out of the examination room without even acknowledging my explanation.

I told the nurse I felt dizzy and needed a place to lie down. The pictures on the wall seemed to spin around. I felt weak and still couldn't believe the doctor had left me there. I asked the nurse if she were trained or anyone there trained in the use of a portable oxygen tank because I felt I may have a seizure because of the blood I'd loss. I'd had rudimentary medical training during my years in the service and knew the signs and consequences of loosing so much blood.

I found myself educating the very people who should have been caring for my emergent health needs. I cautioned her not to be afraid if I did indeed go into shock because I was as harmless as a newborn baby. I told the nurse to administer oxygen, massage me, talk to me and make sure I didn't swallow my tongue. I'm told that right after expressing my concerns and issuing instructions, I went into shock and that the nurse screamed and cried, "Please don't leave us, come back."

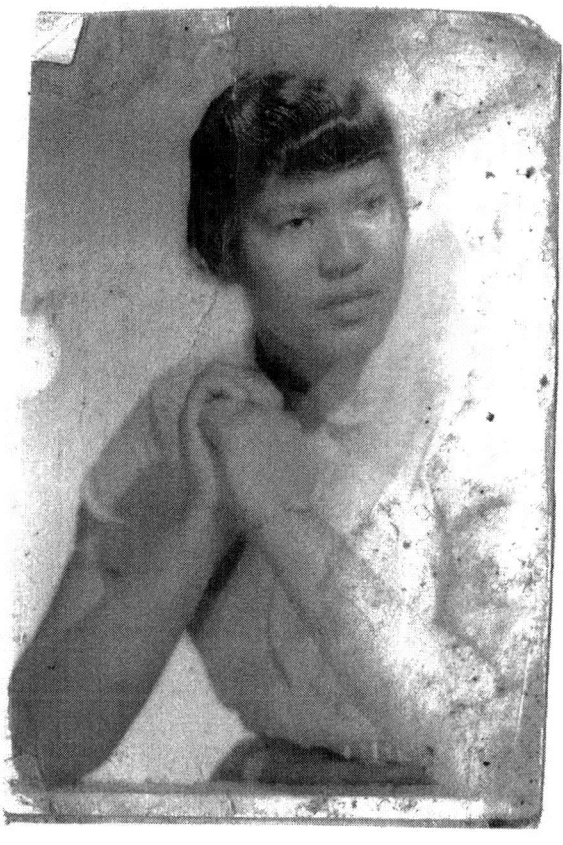

MY SISTER JUANITA

After regaining consciousness, I first thanked God for bringing me back. Most people think when you die, that's it—you just die. I know for a fact that it's more to it than that. I know this because seconds after I went to sleep from the anesthesia, I saw myself dressed in full uniform, knocking on the door of my baby sister, Juanita's home in New Brunswick, New Jersey. My mother, who'd by now was relegated to a wheelchair, lived there in my sister's care. From behind the door I could hear mother say, "I'll be right out baby." And as she opened the door, she was standing upright, without a wheelchair and she appeared decades younger. I truly believe that if God had not brought me back, my mother would have been my sponsor onto the next life.

After I was stabilized, the doctor insisted that I remain there overnight and return to my quarters the next morning. She said that I would be transported to Walter Reed once beds became available. I mustered up enough energy to object and made it clear to her that I was a loyal soldier, but because I felt my life was in danger, I would disobey her orders. "You're not sending me back to my quarters," I insisted. "I'll go to the military police and either have them transport me to Walter Reed or force you to take me there." She seemed hell-bent on harming rather than helping me. The next morning, I was transported directly to Walter Reed. After arriving, I'm told I was given 200cc of blood to stabilize me and medicine for pain and then taken in for various kidney and brain scans.

Later, I noticed several doctor's in my room, some of whom asked me about my service record. I told them of my combat experiences. I also reminded them that even while I was in combat, I always found the time to attend church services because, I felt that any and all requests, prayers and messages I uttered, were sent to God.

The doctor's initially thought they'd spotted brain cancer. Thank God they didn't. They asked if I was ready for the diagnosis. I'd already prepared myself for the worst scenario. They told me there was renal cell cancer in the left kidney. They were also checking whether the cancer had spread.

As I attempted to make out my last will and testament, the witnesses, all female nurses were beginning to tear as I thanked them for their care of me. The head nurse, a member of Oral Robert's church, told me later that she'd been in contact with him and had referenced my story. She said he'd happened to be flying into Washington, D.C. the same night of my surgery and that he assured her that he would intercede with the Almighty on my behalf and that if I kept the faith, I'd be okay. I thanked her.

I also noticed a Thirty-Third Mason, a Protestant minister, a Rabbi and a Catholic priest all present in my room. Maybe it was because I'd told them I'd attended all different services while on duty. A news reporter was also there and asked me what would be on my mind as I went under anesthesia. I said, "the 23rd psalm: 'I will prepare a place for you in the presence of your enemy.'" Had I not recovered, I was told that a story would have been written of my army career in the local paper and New Jersey's main newspaper, The Star Ledger.

The surgery began that evening around 9:00pm and concluded around 12:00am the following day. I had prepared myself mentally for never seeing daylight again. But the next day, one of the doctors said to me, "I know you can't respond to us right now, but I'd like to tell you that He obviously intervened. The cancer hasn't spread." I'd already awakened and had begun silently repeating the 23rd Psalm. He continued with his explanation, explaining that they'd removed the existing cancer. I'd come so close to death once more. One retired Officer approached me and said as a young man he'd served on General Patton's staff. He said, "General Patton would be damn proud of you." All I could think was that life is beautiful.

BAD TÖLZ, GERMANY 1968

After my Vietnam tour, I returned stateside to Fort Bragg, North Carolina. I remained there for about a year and a half before volunteering to return to Europe for the 2nd time joining the 11th Special Forces Group. We were stationed in Bad Tölz, Germany, located in the same area where Adolf Hitler's Commanders had been located, near Munich. I learned that the people in Bad Tölz respected General Patton. His decision not to destroy a much used and needed railroad bridge and overpass was looked upon as a military man of honor. He'd instructed his men instead to open up another method of crossing. Within 5 miles of Bad Tölz sits a mountain where snow remains on top year round. The Sergeant Major in charge of training decided to take about 200 personnel atop the mountain without what I felt, was proper preparation.

There's an African-American proverb that applies to mountain climbing: '*I have got started and I can't turn around.*' During our climb, we encountered a situation that could have proved deadly for all of us. The Sergeant Major seemed to panic, and turned to me to help lead us out of danger. I said to the troops, "We can't turn around, we'll have to continue forward, over the mountain, and hope to find a way off the other side." It was getting dark. The other side of the mountain was steep. As I lead the way, I discovered thick ice on what would be our descent. I decided not to tell the troops and asked God to go with us. I instructed the men to move fast and not look down. When I saw the tops of trees, I said to them, "Once the tree tops come into view, follow me and jump. After landing, run back toward the mountain and hit the ground face down."

When the last group landed, we could see the loose rocks and ice. A huge rock, about the size of a boxcar or larger came crashing down above us, making a noise so loud that it shook the ground and ended up blocking the highway about two thousand yards away. The construction team had to use explosives before they could move it, working most of the night before the main road could reopen. I thanked God for helping me lead all 200 personnel off the mountain.

Due to what I've been through, I don't have any question whether God is real. I have been face-to-face with death so many times and God has saved me and the many people with me. That's the most beautiful part of it all. I'll tell anyone that when death is near, I'm good company to be in.

FORT DEVENS - MASSACHUSETTES

After spending about one year in Germany with the 11th Special Forces Airborne, we were ordered back to the United States in 1969 to Fort Devens, Massachusetts. I remained at Fort Devens for the better part of a year before returning to Fort Dix for about 30 days to complete my 22 years of military service. Presently, the 11th Special Forces is located in Fort Carson, Colorado.

In 1996 I wrote to the department of the Army to volunteer for the Bosnia and Herzegovina conflict but was never called to duty. Today I am still hopeful that my service, duty and contributions will be recognized by the U.S. Army, and am prayerful that one day before I leave this earth that I can say that the Congressional Medal of Honor was no longer forgotten to those of us who were deserving.

MEDALS & RECORD FOR SFC E-7 WILLIAM GIBSON

Distinguished Service Medal
Bronze Star Medal
Meritorious Service Medal
Good Conduct Medal
Master Parachute Badge
GCMDL (3d Award)
CIB 2nd award Korea 1950, Vietnam 1965
Exp (Rifle M1)
AFEM AFEM
AOM (Japan)
AOM (Germany)
NDSM 3 OLC
RVNCM w/60 Device
GCMDL (4th Award)
Army Commendation Medal
Good Conduct Medal
National Defense Service Medal

Vietnam Service Medal
NCO Professional Development Ribbon
Army Service Ribbon
Overseas Service Ribbon (2 Issued)
United Nations Service Medal
Republic of Vietnam Campaign Medal
Presidential Unit Citation
Republic of Korea Presidential Unit Citation
Republic of Vietnam Gallantry Cross Unit Citation
Vietnam Presidential Unit Citation: V (valor) Device
Bronze Arabic Number (2)
CONGRESSIONAL MEDAL of HONOR (?)

WASHINGTON, D.C. 20318-9999

26 April 2000

Mr. William Gibson
251 Commercial Avenue
New Brunswick, NJ 08901

Dear Mr. Gibson,

    It is a pleasure to acknowledge your dedication for more than 50 years of honorable service to the Army and Army Reserve. As a proud member of the Brigade, I was gratified to read about your rejoining our active forces at the age of 61 during Operations DESERT SHIELD and DESERT STORM. Your selfless devotion to duty commands the respect of all Americans.

    Thank you for the courage, loyalty, and commitment that you, along with your comrades in arms, displayed while protecting the freedoms we cherish. Your contributions to our Nation are greatly appreciated.

    With best wishes,

                    Sincerely,

                    HENRY H. SHELTON
                        Chairman
                of the Joint Chiefs of Staff

LETTER FROM HENRY SHELDON
(CHAIRMAN OF THE JOINT CHIEFS OF STAFF)

DEPARTMENT OF THE ARMY
OFFICE OF THE DEPUTY CHIEF OF STAFF FOR PERSONNEL
WASHINGTON, DC 20310-0300

REPLY TO
ATTENTION OF

March 31, 1997

SFC William Gibson, USA (Ret)
251 Commercial Avenue
New Brunswick, New Jersey 08901

Dear Sergeant Gibson:

Thank you for your letter dated December 18, 1996, to the Chairman of the Joint Chiefs of Staff concerning your desire to volunteer for duty in Bosnia and Herzegovina. I have been asked to respond to your letter since the subject you have addressed is within my area of responsibility.

Your request has been forwarded to the U.S. Army Reserve Personnel Center, ATTN: ARPC-MOP-M, 9700 Page Avenue, St. Louis, Missouri 63132-5200, where you will be placed on a list of volunteers. Should the need arise for your particular MOS and rank, you may be contacted.

It is a pleasure to know that you are, once again, willing to answer the call to duty. Your patriotism is truly appreciated.

Sincerely,

Raymond C.V. Robinson, Jr.
Chief of Operations

LETTER FROM RAYMOND C.V. ROBINSON
(CHIEF of OPERATIONS)

CREDO FOR THE SPECIAL SOLDIER

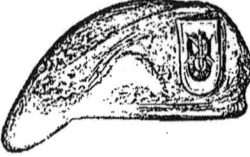

6TH

SFTG

1ST

7TH

I AM THE SPECIAL WARFARE SOLDIER – A SPECIAL KIND OF AMERICAN FIGHTING MAN. MY ROOTS LIE DEEP IN THE HISTORY OF BATTLES – FROM THE CUNNING OF HANNIBAL TO THE WISDOM OF COCHISE, FROM THE ART OF SUN TZU TO THE SKILL OF ROBERT E. LEE. I AM A NEW BREED OF SOLDIER FIGHTING AN OLD KIND OF WAR. THE WORLD HAS CALLED ME BY MANY NAMES – NAMES THAT RESOUND TERROR, NAMES THAT STILL FEAR. MINUTE MAN, GUERRILLA, RANGER, RESISTANCE, OSS, UNDERGROUND, PSYWARRIOR, SERVICE FORCE, MAURAUDER, SPECIAL FORCES. WHENEVER I WAS CALLED, I WAS ALWAYS THERE – AT LEXINGTON AND SHILOH, AT SAN JUAN AND NHA TRANG. YOU CAN HEAR MY SONG IN THE TUNE OF THE FIFE. YOU CAN HEAR MY CRY IN THE TRIUMPH OF THE BUGLE. YOU CAN FEEL MY SPIRIT IN THE BEAT OF THE DRUM. I AM THE ELITE FIGHTING MAN AND MY SKILLS ARE UNSURPASSED. I CAN BUILD A VILLAGE OR DESTROY A CITY. I CAN TRAIN AN ARMY FROM IRREGULARS OR DESTROY AN ARMY OF REGULARS. I CAN HEAL THE SICK OR KILL THE ENEMY. I CAN TRAIN THE MIND FOR GOOD OR CONTROL IT FOR MY CAUSE. I AM GREATER THAN THE MACHINE AND MORE ELUSIVE THAN OUTER SPACE. IN ANY KIND OF WAR, IN ANY EARTHLY PLACE, YOU WILL FIND ME SERVING – IN ANY KIND OF CLIMATE ON ANY TYPE OF TERRAIN. WHETHER IN THE HEAT OF BATTLE OR IN THE COLDNESS OF PEACE, MY JOB IS ALWAYS CONSTANT MY TASK IS NEVER COMPLETE. I AM THE INOCULATION AGAINST DEFEAT AND THE SERUM THAT CURES THE CAUSE OF UNREST. I AM THE FORWARD SHIELD OF THE NATION'S STRENGTH AND THE DISTANT OUTPOST OF FREEDOM'S OFFENSIVE. WHEREVER THE OPPRESSED CRY FOR LIBERATION, WHEREVER THE ENSLAVED YEARN FOR TRUTH AND LIBERTY, WHEREVER DEMOCRACY STRUGGLES FOR THE MIND OF MEN, I, THE SPECIAL WARFARE SOLDIER, AM THERE.

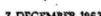

3RD

8TH

7 DECEMBER 1963

WRITTEN AND PRESENTED TO MAJOR GENERAL WILLIAM P. YARBOROUGH, COMMANDING GENERAL OF THE JOHN F. KENNEDY U.S. ARMY CENTER FOR SPECIAL WARFARE, BY MAJOR (CAPTAIN) HAROLD R. SIMS ON THE OCCASION OF HIS DEPARTURE FOR ASSIGNMENT IN SOUTH VIETNAM; (INTENDED AS A PERMANENT EXPRESSION OF THE PERPETUAL CODE OF THE SPECIAL WARFARE SOLDIER AND AS AN OFFERING FOR THE SPECIAL WARFARE MUSEUM.)

5TH

10TH

THE SENATE AND GENERAL ASSEMBLY
STATE HOUSE, TRENTON, N.J.

JOINT LEGISLATIVE RESOLUTION
By Senator SMITH and Assemblymen EGAN and CHIVUKULA

WHEREAS, The Senate and General Assembly of the State of New Jersey are pleased to honor and salute William Gibson, a highly esteemed resident of the Garden State, who is the recipient of the New Brunswick African American Heritage Committee's Trailblazer Award; and,

WHEREAS, This coveted accolade was bestowed upon William Gibson in grateful recognition of his commitment to the United States military and the sacrifices he made for the freedom of the people of this country; and,

WHEREAS, William Gibson served his country with honor and valor as a member of the United States Army during Operation Desert Storm and Operation Desert Shield, achieving the rank of Sergeant First Class and earning several awards and commendations; and,

WHEREAS, William Gibson's great sacrifice for the causes of freedom and democracy will never be forgotten by his family, his State, and his country; and,

WHEREAS, Within all the spheres of his life and work, William Gibson has established a model to emulate and set a standard of excellence toward which others might strive; and,

WHEREAS, It is altogether proper and fitting for this Legislature to commend William Gibson as an individual of outstanding character and exceptional determination; now, therefore,

Be It Resolved by the Senate and General Assembly of the State of New Jersey:

That this Legislature hereby joins the New Brunswick African American Heritage Committee in honoring and saluting William Gibson as a recipient of the Trailblazer Award, pays tribute to his meritorious record of military service, and extends to him this Legislature's sincere best wishes; and,

Be It Further Resolved, That a duly authenticated copy of this resolution, signed by the Senate President and the Assembly Speaker and attested by the Senate Secretary and the Assembly Clerk, be transmitted to William Gibson.

Attest:

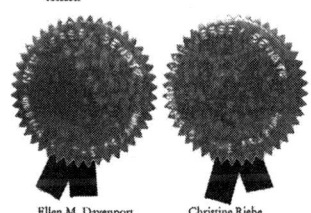

Ellen M. Davenport
Secretary of the Senate

Christine Riehe
Clerk of the General Assembly

President of the Senate

Speaker of the General Assembly

DOCUMENT FROM THE SENATE AND GENERAL ASSEMBLY